ON

THE COINS

OF THE

PATAN SULTANS OF HINDUSTAN

ON

THE COINS

OF THE

PATAN SULTANS OF HINDUSTAN.

BY

EDWARD THOMAS, ESQ.

GYAN

Published by

Gyan Publishing House
5, Ansari Road
Daryaganj, New Delhi-110002
Phone: 011-47034999, 9811692060
E-mail: books@gyanbooks.com

Distribution Network
gyanbooks.com
India, USA, Canada, UK, Australia, France

ISBN: 978-81-212-7785-3 (PB)
First Published, 1847

2nd Impression 2023

Printed at: Gyan Press, Delhi.

ON THE COINS OF THE PATAN SULTANS OF HINDUSTAN
Author: EDWARD THOMAS

ON

THE COINS

OF THE

PATAN SULTANS OF HINDUSTAN.

أَطِيعُوا اللّٰهَ وَأَطِيعُوا الرَّسُولَ وَأُولِي الأَمْرِ مِنْكُمْ

KORAN, Surah iv., ver. 62. (Coin No. 101.)

BY

EDWARD THOMAS, ESQ.,

BENGAL CIVIL SERVICE;

MEM. ROYAL ASIATIC SOCIETY, AND MEM. NUMISMATIC SOCIETY, LONDON.

LONDON:

PRINTED BY J. WERTHEIMER AND CO., FINSBURY CIRCUS.

1847.

PREFACE.

THE history of Mohammedan nations is for many reasons peculiarly suitable for numismatic illustration; not so much in reference to the artistic value of the coins themselves, as from the fact of their usually recording in full the name of the king, the date, and the place of coinage thus affording direct evidence to three distinct points,—the existence of the sovereign as such, the time in which he reigned, and the place of which he was king.

The value of this species of illustration, as applied to Indian history, is much enhanced by the consideration of the oriental feeling, that the power of coinage was held to be a proof of the attainment of kingly dignity. In the West, we require many forms to make a king, but the Eastern Mohammedan races seem to have held the striking of the currency, aided by an immediate recitation of public prayers in the names of the princes they had elected, as proof positive of sovereignty. Thus we find the first act of an Eastern reign was invariably the production of a coin; without this, an all-powerful despot hardly felt himself a king.

The medals of Eastern kings, unlike the money of European nations, were really the coins of the sovereign whose name they recorded; they were less the money of the country than a part of the wealth of the king himself. The despotism which enabled the ruler to alter at will the circulating medium of his dominions, identifies the coinage itself most intimately with the monarch who issued it; hence, from these metallic records, we can often trace, not only historical facts, but even the workings of men's minds ; at least the results of their vices or virtues are frequently to be detected in the silent testimonies they have left behind them. As an instance, the history of few reigns offers such varied numismatic illustrations as that of Mohammed bin Tuglak. Amid the endless variety, and at times perfection of execution, of his medals, we discover a register of all the phases of his rule—his early wealth and profusion, his subsequent poverty, and his despotic endeavour to meet it: the one witnessed in the quantity and full weight of his first coinage; succeeded, on the other hand, by the currency of debased metal, ending in the issue of copper tokens which he attempted to pass in lieu of silver. Next we note his forced return to honesty and its consequent effect upon his money; the religious scruples which overtook him in 743 A.H. are also evidenced in his coins, when, after having, in imitation of his predecessors, barely recognised the existence of a Khalif, he is suddenly alarmed by doubts as to his own right to the throne of Hindustan, unsupported as it was by the sanction of a Commander of the faithful. Then, not satisfied with acknowledging the spiritual supremacy of a Khalif whose name was scarcely known, he at once (entirely rejecting his own titles) stamps his currency with the name of Al Mustakfí billah (the supposed Khalif of Egypt). The medals of subsequent years indicate the recognition of his title to the throne of Delhí by Al Abbás Ahmed the successor of Al Mustakfí.

The period which our series of medals illustrates, extends

from A.D. 1192 to 1554, three centuries and a half. During this time, five dynasties, numbering in all forty kings, succeeded each other on the throne of Delhí. We are fortunate in this pēriod, following the exact point of Indian history where Professor H. H. Wilson closes his labors in his Ariana Antiqua, he having, somewhat *per saltum* indeed, brought down Indian numismatics from the time of Alexander the Great to the commencement of the Patán rule in Hindustan.

In the weight and device of the gold and silver coins of the early Patán kings, but little variation is to be observed from the commencement of the series until the reign of Mohammed bin Tuglak the nineteenth sovereign on our list. The gold coins up to this last date, judging from specimens of the mintage of Balban and Mohammed Sháh were usually denominated سكه *Sicca*, a die (a coin), a word probably used only in the generic sense. The greatest weight of the above pieces, is 172 grains; but we have a Ghiás ed dín Tuglak as high as 173 grains. The silver coins were termed الفضة *Al-fazzat*, the silver (coin), and at times merely *Sicca*. The weight of these ranges up to 173 grains. For both these classes of medals, allowing for wear, we may fairly assume a mint issue of 174 grains. A curious description of coin now brings itself to our notice, being a sort of medium currency between copper and silver, composed, indeed, of a mixture of these two metals. However objectionable this intermediate coinage may appear in theory, there are many advantages to be conceded to it in practice. In a poor country where great subdivision of the currency was found necessary, it was a manifest convenience to convert so small a mite of silver, as $\frac{1}{16}$ of a Dirhem (10·8 grains) into something tangible, at the same time a pure copper representative of this sum would have been bulky and unmanageable. Under any circumstances some proof of the advantage of this admixture of metals, is to be found in the fact of its having continued in use upwards of four centuries and a half, dating from Anungpál of Lahore, A.D. 1000, with whom this species of coin seems to have originated, through the early Delhí imitators of the Kábúl coinage to the time of Behlól Lodí, A.D. 1450.

These coins, like those of gold and silver of the same kings, underwent but little change from the accession of Mohammed bin Sám, to the time of Mohammed bin Tuglak. They average, as will be seen from the weights affixed to each engraved specimen, from 52 to 56 grains: of this, the native refiners calculate from 10 to 11 grains to be silver.

The simple copper coins usually weigh 55 grains up to the reign of Balban, whose copper pieces, and those of his successors, rise as high as 66 and 67 grains.

Mubárik Sháh adopted the square form for many of his coins, without, however, varying the weights or values.

Mohammed bin Tuglak, in addition to debasing the coinage in every possible way, and attempting to pass copper tokens in lieu of silver money, seems from the first to have altered the whole system of the currency in a most unaccountable manner. On the one hand, we find his early gold coins of the year 726, A.H. (denominated Dínars), brought up to the weight of 200 grains, whereas his silver coins of the same type, are let down from the old standard of 174 grains, to 140 odd. His debased thick silver Dirhems of the years 727, 28, 29, and 30, average, even in nearly perfect specimens, only 139 grains. His small silver Quarter-Dirhems, again, appear to have remained unaltered, at least in point of weight; while his brass and copper money, on the other hand, displays an endless variety of shape, weight and device. Fírúz III. reverted to the old standard for his gold coinage, though the types and inscriptions vary considerably. His debased silver, or silver and copper coins, whichever we may take them to be, seem to have been imitated from the thick silver money of Mohammed bin Tuglak, and to have been continued by Fírúz and his successors, but little changed, either in weight or purity of metal, down to Behlól Lodí, the thirty-third sultan on our list. We have specimens of the silver coinage of Mohammed bin Fírúz and Máhmúd bin Mohammed, evincing, in their worn state, a probable original mint-weight of the old 174 grains. It is remarkable, considering the manifold coins of other metal, of the fifteen kings who followed Mohammed bin Tuglak, that are now extant, how very few silver medals of these princes have as yet come to light. The copper coinage of the period intervening between the reigns of Mohammed bin Tuglak and Shír Sháh, does not offer any change worthy of remark. This last sovereign entirely remodelled the coinage of his dominions: his silver money, now for the first time denominated rupee, is stated by James Prinsep to have weighed 11¼ *mashas* of 15·5 grains, i.e. 174·4 grains. This weight is, however, easily proved to be too little, as Marsden has already published rupees of this king rising from 177 to 178 grains. The coins also of Shír's immediate successors, Islám and Ádil, frequently weigh as much as 176 and 177 grains. Under these circumstances, and allowing for wear and loss from other causes, we shall be justified in rating the weight of these rupees, at the time of issue, at 178, if not at the full *tolah* of 180 grains. Shír Sháh's larger copper coinage runs as high as 316 grains; and the smaller pieces average 150 and 40 grains respectively.

The present series, it will be seen, is very complete, being wanting in the coins of four kings only out of the forty. The absence or non-existence of the money of these monarchs is perhaps easily accounted for, and will be noticed at large in its proper place.

By far the major part of this collection is as yet unpublished, and, with a view to avoid the imperfection which omissions would cause, some few coins which have already appeared have been re-produced: but in nearly every case the engravings have been taken from originals other than those hitherto made public. Closing this brief introductory notice, it is proposed at once to proceed to describe the medals themselves, prefixing to the whole a full list of the Sultáns and their dates of accession; introducing subsequently in detail a transcript and translation of the Persian inscription to be found on the coins of each succeeding monarch, preceded by a short note of the most prominent occurrences of the reign.

LIST OF THE PATÁN, AFGHÁN OR GHORÍ SULTANS OF HINDÚSTÁN (DELHÍ).

Date of Accession. A.H.	A.D.	No. of King.	
589	1193	1	Muaz ud din, or Shaháb ud din Mohammed bin Sám (1st Dynasty).
602	1205	2	Kutb ud din Ibek.
607	1210	3	Arám Sháh bin Ibek.
—	1211	4	Shums ud din Altumsh.
633	1236	5	Ruckn ud din Fírúz Sháh (Fírúz I.).
634	——	6	Sultán Rezíah.
637	1239	7	Muaz ud din Behrám Sháh.
639	1241	8	Alá ud din Masáud Sháh.
644	1246	9	Násir ud din Mahmúd.
664	1266	10	Ghiás ud din Balban.
685	1286	11	Muaz ud din Kaikobád.
687	1288	12	Jellál ud din Fírúz Sháh (Fírúz II.), (2nd Dynasty, Khiljí).
695	1295	13	Rukn ud din Ibrahím.
—	——	14	Alá ud din Mohammed Sháh.
716	1316	15	Shaháb ud din Umur.
717	1317	16	Kutb ud din Mubárik Sháh I.
721	1321	17	Násir ud din Khusrú.
—	——	18	Ghiás ud din Tuglak Sháh (3rd Dyn. Tuglak).
725	1325	19	Mohammed bin Tuglak.
752	1351	20	Fírúz Sháh bin Salar Rajab (Fírúz III.).
790	1388	21	Ghiás ud din Tuglak Sháh II.
791	1389	22	Abúbekir Sháh.
793	1390	23	Násir ud din Mohammed Sháh bin Fírúz Sháh.
796	1394	24	Alá ud din Sekunder Sháh (named Humáyún).
—	——	25	Násir ud din Mahmúd Sháh bin Mohammed Sháh (Tímúr, 800).
797	1395	26	Nuserut Sháh (Interregnum). Mahmúd restored 802.

Date of Accession A.H.	A.D.	No. of King	
814	1412	27	Daulut Khán Lodí.
817	1414	28	Khizr Khán (4th Dynasty, Syuds).
824	1421	29	Muaz ud din Mubárik Sháh (II.).
839	1435	30	Mohammed Sháh bin Feríd Sháh.
849	1444	31	Alá ud din bin Mohammed.
854	1450	32	Behlól Lodí (5th Dynasty, Lodí).
894	1488	33	Sekunder bin Behlól.
923	1517	34	Ibrahím bin Sekunder (Báber, 930 H.).
937	1530	35	Mohammed Humáyún (Moghul).
947	1540	36	Feríd ud din Shír Sháh.
952	1545	37	Islám Sháh.
960	1553	38	Mohammed Ádil Sháh.
961	——	39	Ibrahím Súr.
962	1554	40	Sekunder Sháh (Humáyún, 962, then Akber).

Preliminary Note.

The slight historical notices at the head of the medals of each king, consisting of little more than extracts from Ferishtah, have been inserted in the desire of avoiding continual references to histories of the time. In acknowledging the use made of the works of Briggs and Elphinstone, we cannot do better than refer to them for fuller details than our space admits of. The list of kings, somewhat modified, has been taken from the tables published by the Asiatic Society of Bengal. The Hijra dates have been retained as being in themselves more appropriate to the subject, and as affording a more direct correspondence with the dates to be found on the coins.

It is to be noticed, in referring to the plates, that in the present series of medals, in which the legends read from right to left, the obverse face has been made to take the place usually assigned to the reverse in engravings of European coins.

The very limited number of collections of the class of

coins here described does not admit of any attempt at refinement in expressing the rarity of the different specimens. The most common marks of C., R., V. R., and Unique, have alone therefore been made use of, and these only in reference to the more important medals.

Where an inscription has been restored in full, as in the case of the legend on the outer circle of the obverse of No. 1, the lines above serve to show the words which are to be found in the specimen engraved.

As an English translation of the titles of the kings would interfere with the facility of identification of the individual, who is often better known by his titular designation than by his specific name, and as the strict English rendering of these epithets themselves usually sounds inflated, and, in many instances, absurd, it has been thought desirable to avoid doing more than anglicising the original denominations. It may be sufficient to indicate generally that the titles usually have reference to the religious and temporal celebrity each king at the time of his accession hoped to attain.

First King (A.H. 589—602; A.D. 1193—1206).

Shaháb ud din, or Muaz ud din Mohammed bin Sám, known also by the title of Mohammed Ghorí, the founder of the Patán dynasty of Delhí, is first noticed in history on the occasion of his appointment, in conjunction with his brother, Ghiás ud din, to the government of a province of Ghor, by his uncle, the notorious Alá ud din, the destroyer of Guzní. After the accession of Ghiás ud din to the throne of Ghor in 554 H., Muaz ud din, acting as his general, subdued Khorassan; and, on the conquest of Guzní from Khusrú Malik, in 567, he was nominated to the government of that country. From this time his incursions into

India commenced: in 572, he conquers Multán; in 574, he meets with a sanguinary defeat in an expedition against the prince of Guzrat; in 575, and in 580, Khusrú, the last of the Guznívedes, now king of Lahore, is assailed; and, at length, in 582, subdued by stratagem. In 587, in a more extended expedition into Hindústán, Mohammed Ghorí is totally routed on the memorable field of Thanésur, by the Chohán hero, Prithví, rajah of Ajmír and Delhí. After two years' repose, the disgrace of his defeat still burning within him, he, on the self-same battle ground, again encounters his former conqueror, who is now supported by the whole force of the country, the confederated armies of 150 princes. This time victory favours the Ghorians, and a hard-fought field ends in the total discomfiture of the Indian host. By this single victory the Mohammedans may be said to have become the virtual masters of Hindústán. The ulterior measures for the subjugation of the rest of the country were of speedy accomplishment, and most of the later additions to the Indian empire of Mohammed Ghorí were perfected by his quondam slave, subsequent representative in Hindústán, and eventual successor on the throne of Delhi, Kutb ud din Ibek. Ghiás ud din, who had long retained little beyond the title of a king, died in 600, H.; and, shortly afterwards, Muaz ud din was crowned in form. An unsuccessful attempt at conquest in the north, in itself attended by most disastrous consequences, was succeeded by the revolt of the governors of Guzní and Multán: this outbreak, however, was soon suppressed. In 602, Mohammed Ghorí was slain in his tent, in the centre of his own camp, by a band of his Indian subjects, who thus avenged the loss they had sustained in the wars he had inflicted upon their country. At the death of Mohammed Ghorí, the Mohammedan empire in India extended generally over nearly the whole of Hindústán Proper, Sindh, and Bengal. The sovereignty was, however, held by various tenures, and was most uncertain in its internal geographical limits.

1.—Silver. 74 grs. V.R. A.H. 596. (*Prinsep Collection.*)

Obv.—

هو الذی ارسل رسوله بالهدی ودین الحق لیظهره علی الدین کله
ولو کره المشرکون
لا اله الا الله محمد رسول الله السلطان الاعظم
غیاث الدنیاو الدین ابو الفتح
محمد بن سام

R.—

ضرب هذا الدرهم فی بلده غزنه بسنه سته و تسعین و خمس مایة
الناصر لدین الله السلطان المعظم معز
الدنیا و الدین ابو المظفر
محمد بن سام

TRANSLATION.

Obv.—It is he that sendeth his messenger, with guidance and true faith, that he might exalt the (true) religion above all, though the infidels be averse thereto.—There is no god but God. Mohammed is the prophet of God! The most mighty sovereign,—Ghiás ud dunia wa ud din, Abúlfateh. —Mohammed bin Sám.

R.—This Dirhem (was) struck in the city of Ghazneh, in the year Five hundred and ninety-six.—Al Násir le din illah.[1] The mighty sovereign, Muaz—ud dunia wa ud din Abúl Muzafar.—Mohammed bin Sám.

2.—Silver. 68 grs. R.

Obv.—

الله محمد رسول الله السلطان المعظم معز الدنیا و الدین ابو
المظفر محمد بن سام

[1] The name of the khalif.

Margin.—

ضرب هذا الدر سنه اربع و مايه

℞.—

الله لا اله الا الله الناصر بالله السلطان الا عظم غياث الدنيا والدين

ابو الفتح محمد بن سام

Margin.—و لو كره المشركون &c., same as No. 1, *obv. margin.*

TRANSLATION.

Obv.—God. Mohammed is the prophet of God. The mighty Sultan, Muaz ud dunia wa ud din, the victorious Mohammed bin Sám.

Margin.—This Dirhem (was) struck . . . . year . . and four

℞.—God. There is no god but God. Al nasir billah. The most mighty Sultan, Ghiás ud dunia wa ud din, the victorious Mohammed bin Sám.

Margin.—Same as No. 1.

N.B. There is a gold coin in the Masson collection, weighing 99 grs., similar in size and shape to this silver Dirhem. It is in bad preservation, and the inscriptions are scarcely legible.

The above coins in the joint names of Ghiás and Muaz ud din, bear testimony to the associated regal powers of the two brothers. It is to be noticed, however, that the superlative الا عظم "The greatest," is applied to the one king, while معظم "Great," is all that is extended to the conqueror of India. It will be observed from the coins which follow, that, on the death of his brother, Muaz ud din took to himself the superlative الا عظم

A more intricate question is, however, suggested by the legends on these coins, in regard to the identity of Mohammed bin Sám himself. It will be seen from the transcript above given, that in one place is to be found the title of

Ghiás ud din, and in another the epithet of Muaz ud din, each in conjunction with the name of Mohammed bin Sám.

Up to the present time, Muaz ud din, otherwise in all written history styled Shaháb ud din, has invariably been identified as Mohammed bin Sám, or Mohammed Ghorí; but the inscriptions on our coins would indicate that if Muaz ud din is *Mohammed bin Sám*, so also is Ghiás ud din.

The coins of Mahmúd, the son of Ghiás ud din, the nephew and Afghán successor of Muaz ud din, distinctly proclaim the king who issued them the son of Mohammed bin Sám (vide foot of page 99).

The necessary inference from this evidence is that Ghiás ud din owned the name of Mohammed; and as all are prepared to admit Muaz ud din's claim to that designation, there is nothing left but to conclude that both brothers bore or assumed the generally favourite appellation of Mohammed.

Should the legends of the medals themselves be considered as insufficient proof of the strength of the position now assumed, it may be as well to advert to any readily accessible *written* evidence which may serve to throw a light on the question.

Price, in his Mohammedan History,[2] on the authority of the "Khalásut ul Akhbár," calls Ghiás ud din, *Mohammed bin Sám*; leaving Shaháb ud din undesignated beyond this title, and an allusion to his parentage as derived from Sám.

The accuracy of the translation of the passage referred to is fully confirmed by a reference to an original MS. of the Khalásut ul Akhbár in the Library of the Royal Asiatic

---

[2] Vol. ii. p. 455.

Society;[3] and the correctness of the purport of the text of the work in question is directly upheld and more fully explained by the following passage from the Rozsut us Safá.[4]

و به استصواب اشراف آن دیار سلطان غیاث الدین‌را برتخت نشاند و قبل از سلطنت محمد بن سام‌را شمس الدین میگفتند و برادرش شهاب الدین میخواندند چون بر سریر جهانداری تمکن یافت ملقب بسلطان غیاث الدین گشت و برادرش‌را معز الدین لقب دادند

"And with the approbation of the nobles of that country (he) placed Sultan Ghiás ud din on the throne. Prior to his accession, Mohammed bin Sám was called Shums ud din, and his brother was designated Shaháb ud din; (but) when he became king, he became entitled Ghiás ud din, and his brother was surnamed Muaz ud din."

The conclusion above suggested, if not entirely borne out, is very strongly supported by the application of the designations of Mohammed to both brothers, in an earlier part of the last mentioned work, on the first introductory notice of their names on the occasion of their imprisonment by Alá ud din.

3.—Silver. 71 grs. R.

Obv.—

السّلطان الا عظم معز الدنیا و الدین ابو المظفر محمّد بن سام

Margin.— ضرب هذا الدرهم شهور

[3] No. 101, MS. Catalogue. See also, Mirát al Alem, No. 55, idem.

[4] Mír Kháwand, known as Mírkhond. MS. Catalogue, No. 43, Library of the Asiatic Society.

R.—

لا اله الا الله محمد رسول الله الناصر لدين الله امير المومنين

Margin.—

هو الذی ارسـ و دين الحق ليظهره ی الدين كله

TRANSLATION.

Obv.—The most mighty sovereign, Muaz ud dunia wa ud din, The victorious Mohammed bin Sám.

Margin.—This Dirhem was struck . . . months . .

R.—There is no god but God. Al násir le din illah, The commander of the faithful.

Margin.—Imperfect, same as No. 1 *obv. margin.*

A similar medal, in the possession of Dr. Swiney, has the date 598.

The Guzní coins of the above class, in the sole name of Muaz ud din Mohammed bin Sám, were most probably issued after the death of Ghiás ud din; they are remarkable in having apparently served as models, in point of form, for the silver money of the succeeding kings of Delhi.

4.—Mixed copper and silver. 49 grs. R.

Obv.—السلطان الا عظم محمد بن سام

The most mighty Sultan, Mohammed bin Sám.

R.—Horseman in outline, and श्री हमीरः Sri Hamírah (Amír).[5]

5.—Mixed Copper and Silver. 49 grs.

Obv.—Same as No. 4.

R.—Rude figure of a cavalier.

6.—Silver (impure). 46 grs.

Obv.—السلطان الاعظم ابوالمظفر محمد بن سام

The most mighty Sultan, The victorious Mohammed bin Sám.

R.—The same as No. 5.

---

[5] A Devanágrí abbreviation of the full Arabic title of *Amír Al Mominín*, The commander of the faithful.

7.—Silver and Copper. R.

Obv.—السلطان المعظم معز الدنيا و الدين

R.—محمد بن سام

8.—Silver and Copper. 46 grs.

Obv.—السلطان المعظم معز الدنيا و الدين

R.—ابو المظفر محمد بن سام

9.—Silver and Copper. 49 grs. C.

Obv.—सा महमद सामे Sa (Shah) Mahamad Same.

R.—श्री हमीरः Sri Hamirah.

10.—Silver and Copper. 46 grs. C.

Obv.—महमद सामि Mahamad Sami.

R.—Horseman.

Though not strictly to be classed among the coins of the Mohammedan kings of India, it may not be inappropriate to notice in this place, with reference to the title of Mohammed bin Sám, the following unique unpublished medal of Táj ud din Ilduz, the governor of Guzní, who attempted to throw off his allegiance on his master's defeat in Khwarizm.

This coin, in weight 96 grs., has on its obverse, السلطان المعز The Sultan Al Muaz, in a small square area; and on its broad margin, the legend السلطاني عبد و مولا تاج الدنيا و الدين يلدز The royal servant and slave, Táj ud dunia wa ud din Ilduz. The reverse has the same inscription as No. 3, but the date on the margin is unfortunately wanting. The copper coins of this governor (who subsequently became king of Guzní) are common, and a specimen, struck in the time of Mohammed bin Sám, may be referred to in No. 18, pl. xx., Ariana Antiqua.

Before dismissing the subject of the coins of Mohammed Ghorí, a reference should be made to certain specimens of what is known as the later Kanoúj coinage bearing the name of Mohammed bin Sám and Mír Mohammed Sám, in Hindí. These medals are given in detail in Professor Wilson's Ariana Antiqua (pl. xx., figs. 25, 26, 27, and 27 suppl. pl.) It has not been thought necessary to reproduce these coins in the present notice of the money of the Patán sultans, as, from the absence of the names of any other kings in our list, it is evident the medals in question were merely a temporary continuation of the local mintage on the first conquest of the country by the Mohammedans.

SECOND KING (A.H. 602—607; A.D. 1206—1210).

From the actual accession of Kutb ud din Ibek, in 602 A.H., till his death in 607, with the exception of his conquest of Guzní from Ilduz, and its subsequent loss, but little worthy of note occurred; and the empire remained much in the state to which he himself may be said to have brought it prior to his investiture with the emblems of kingly dignity by Mahmúd, the nephew and Afghán successor[6] of Mohammed Ghorí.

Kutb ud din, while acting as viceroy for Mohammed bin Sám, may be supposed to have issued the money of his government in the name of his master. Nos. 8 and 9 bear signs of being the produce of the Delhí mint, and are probably some of the coins produced under Kutb ud din's auspices. The oriental reverence attaching to the right to coin militates against an inference that Ibek struck no money in his own name; at the same time, it is possible that his experience in the realities of kingly power, before

[6] The copper money of this prince, in form and weight and device, similar to the coin No. 4, bears the following legend:— السلطان الاعظم محمود بن محمد بن سام The most mighty Sultan, Mahmud bin Mohammed bin Sám.

he arrived at the nominal rank of an independent sovereign, may have rendered him careless of the mere forms of royalty; among which last is most certainly to be classed an issue of coin, for the sole purpose of proving the existence of the power of coining.

The coin attributed by Marsden to this king is from the mint of Kutb ud din Mubárik.

Third King (a.h. 607; a.d. 1210—1211).

Arám succeeded his father, Ibek; but after a reign of barely one year, during which he lost many of the provinces of his kingdom, he was defeated and deposed by Altumsh, at that time governor of Budáon.

11.—Copper. 54 grs. V.R.

Obv.—ابو المظفر ارام شاه السلطان The victorious Arám Shah, the Sultan.

℞.—Rude figure of a cavalier.

12.—Copper.

Obv.—Idem.

Owing to the paucity of specimens (two only being known), their bad preservation, and wretched execution, it is difficult to feel assured of the correct attribution of the above coins: suffice it to say, the identification is sanctioned by all orientalists who have been consulted on the subject.

Fourth King (a.h. 607—633; a.d. 1211—1236).

Shums ud din Altumsh, like Ibek, had originally been a slave; rising, however, to be general and son-in-law to his master, he finally displaced that master's son. From his accession, in 607, with the exception of his victory over Ilduz, who was in possession of Guzní and other provinces, and an attempt to subdue his brother-in-law, Kubá Chah,[7] king of Sindh, his reign was, for the time, comparatively tranquil, and remained undisturbed even by the threatened advance of the Moguls under Zengiz Khán. In 622 he finally overcame Kubá Chah, and re-attached Sindh to the empire. During this year, the governor of Bengal and Behar was brought to acknowledge the supremacy of the monarch of Delhí, which had been disclaimed by Baktiar Khíljí since the death of Ibek. The sultan was employed for the next six years in the subjection of those portions of the country which had remained independent, or, having been conquered, had revolted; and, before his death, Altumsh ruled over all Hindústán, with the exception of some few insulated portions. The powers of Mohammedan sultans, as rulers, as indeed those of all lordships of Hindústán, from its earliest history, seem to have been most indeterminate: at times, and in certain districts, extending to absolute possession of soil and people on the part of the king, and full and perfect subjection on the part of the local governors and those they ruled over; liable however at any time to endless fluctuations, as the strength of the sovereign, the turbulence of the governor, or the spirit of independence of the people, rose or fell. In other cases, allegiance reached only so far as a nominal recognition of supremacy, or even a tacit abstinence from denial of such; suffice it to say, that among the multifarious

---

[7] For coins of this prince, vide Ariana Antiqua, fig. 19, pl. xx.; Journal of the Asiatic Society, Bengal, vol. iv. figs. 47, 28, 29, pl. xxxvii. The inscriptions on these pieces may be read as follows: Nos. 19 and 47—*Obv.* ناصر الدنیا و الدین قباچه السلطان Násir ud dunia wa ud din Kubá Chah, a Sultan. ℞.—Horseman and श्री हमीर. And Nos. 28 and 29—*Obv.* The bull Nandí and श्री कुपाचहा सुलतां (Sri Kupáchahá Sultan). ℞.—Same as Nos. 19 and 47.

tenures, and the many changes it was constantly liable to, one general rule of absolute monarchy prevailed—that the length of the sword was the limit of the sway. During the course of Altumsh's reign, he received investiture from the Khalif of Baghdad—a most important recognition to a Mohammedan government, and one that is remarkable as being the earliest notice taken by the court of Baghdad of this new Indo-Mohammedan kingdom. Mohammed bin Sám, though he adopted the titles of the khalifs on his coins, did so probably not so much with reference to his Indian kingdom as on the strength of being the successor to the throne of Guzní; the monarchs of which dynasty had for centuries been acknowledged as faithful Mussulmans, and their subjects considered as part of the flock of The Commander of the Faithful. The Indian conquests constituted, during the lifetime of Mohammed bin Sám, only a portion of the whole Guzní empire. Shortly after his death, however, when the Indian provinces were erected into a separate kingdom, they ceased to have any dependence on the rulers of the countries whence the race of their new kings had come. Altumsh died in 634, and was succeeded by his son.

13.—Silver. 164 grs. R. (*Prinsep Collection.*)[8]

Obv.—السلطان الا عظم شمس الدنيا و الدين ابو المظفر التمش السلطان The most mighty Sultan, Shums ud dunia wa ud din abúl Muzuffir Altumsh, the Sultan.

---

[8] Neither Oriental authors nor Indian moneyers seem to have had any very definite idea of the correct orthography of the name of this king. Rashid ud din, Mirkhond, and the author of the Khalásut ul Akhbár, all differ slightly in their mode of spelling this word; and the masters of the Delhí mint will be seen to have been as little particular. The indecision of these last is somewhat to be excused, seeing the Túrkí origin of the title in question,

℞.—لا اله الا الله محمد رسول الله المستنصر بالله امير المومنين There is no god but God, Mohammed is the prophet of God. Al Mustansir billah, the Commander of the Faithful.

Marg.—ضرب هذا الدر - - - مايه

A second specimen (Lord Auckland's) has the same obverse, but a different reverse, and the inscriptions on both sides are in squares within circles.

℞.—Area - - في عهد الامام المستنصر امير المومنين

In the time of Al Mustansir, the Commander of the Faithful.

Marg.—ضرب هذه النقرة - - - ستمايه

14.—Silver. 53 grs. V.R.

Obv.—श्री सुलतां लितितिमिसि सं १२८३ Sri Sultan Lititimisi sun, 1283 (Sumvut, 1283; A.H. 623).

℞.—In circle, السلطان ايلتمش Sultan Aeltumsh.

15.—Silver and Copper. 48 grs. C.

Obv.—असावरी श्री समसोरल्दिवि Bull and Asáwurí srí Sămăsórăldivi.

℞.—सी चाहरदिव Sri Cháhar div. Horseman.

The clear cutting of the die of the above coin, and the number of specimens of a similar character it is possible to refer to,[9] leave no doubt as to the correct reading of the inscription on the obverse, Asáwurí sri Sămăsórăldíví. The legend on the reverse however presents a slight difficulty, incident to the transition state of the Devanágrí alphabet, in the initial letter of the name. It has been proposed to read this as R or V; but the occurrence of both these con-

---

which, Col. Briggs has shown, was derived from the Túrkí word التمش Sixty, at which number of Tomans our slave king was heretofore purchased.

[9] Ariana Antiqua, pl. xix., figs. 16, 31, 34, 37.

sonants in the latter part of the name itself, where they are found differing in shape from the letter in question, makes this rendering inadmissible.

In regard to the coin itself, there is reason to suppose that it derives its origin from the mint of some *Hindú* prince, as a reference to the Hindú creed seems to be signified in the use of the word Asáwurí, as well as by the fact that coins having the same reverse are extant, bearing the old Brahmanical name of Srí Samanta dev, in the place here taken possession of by the title of Sri Shums ud din.

It may therefore be taken to be the sample of the money of some Hindú ruler, who, once independent, became subsequently subject to the arms or policy of Altumsh; the emperor, in upholding the local sovereignty of his new vassal, probably obliged him to acknowledge the supremacy of his lord paramount, by inscribing the imperial titles on the currency he was still allowed to issue.

The name of Cháhur dev is a known one in the family of the last Hindú king of Delhí, and was borne by a brother of Prithví Rajah himself, as well as (if Abul Fazl is to be trusted) by an immediate predecessor of this prince on the throne of the Chohans at Ajmír.

16.—Silver and Copper. 48 grs. C.

Obv.—सलतण सा समसदीं Sŭltăn să sŭmăsă dín. Bull.

R.—श्री हमीर Sri Hămīrăh. Horseman.

17.—Silver and Copper. 46 grs. C.

Obv.—شمس الدنيا و الدين اليتمش Shums ud dunia wa ud din Aletumsh.

R.—Horseman and Sri Hămírăh.

18.—Silver and Copper. 53 grs. C.

Obv.—شمس الدنيا و الدين اليتمش السلطان Shums ud dunia wa ud din Aletumsh, the Sultan.

R.—Horseman and Sri Hămírăh.

19.—Copper. 26 grs. R.

Obv.—السلطان The Sultan.

℞.—عدل Just.

20.—Copper. 24 grs. C.

Obv.—عدل سلطان The just Sultan.

℞.—بحضرت دهلي (Struck) at the capital, Delhi.

21.—Copper. 28 grs. R.

Obv.—شمس Shums.

℞.—श्री समस दीन Sri Sămăs dín.

22.—Copper. 25½ grs. R.

Obv.—عدل The Just.

℞.—شمس Shums.

23.—Copper. 25½ grs.

Obv.—سلطان Sultan.

℞.—التمش Altumsh.

There is a silver coin in the Prinsep Cabinet, weighing 163 grs., inscribed: *Obv.*—لا اله الا الله محمد رسول الله *Rev.*—في عهد الامام المستنصر امير المومنين which will probably be found to be a medal of Altumsh, struck on the arrival of the diploma of the khalif, recognising the independent Mohammedan empire of Delhi. In the absence of any name except that of the khalif, and in the total loss of the marginal legends, it is of course impossible to decide with certainty to whom this coin belongs. However, the style, the shape of the letters, the khalif's title, and particularly those titles standing alone, all justify the supposition regarding its origin which is now advanced.

Fifth King (a.h. 633—634; a.d. 1237—1238).

Ruckn ud din Fírúz's unimportant reign of seven months' duration was terminated by the elevation of his sister, the celebrated Rezíah.

24, 25, 26.—Copper. 55 and 42 grs. V.R.

Obv.—السّلطان المعظم ركن الدين بن السّلطان The great King, Rukn ud din, son of the Sultan.

ꝶ.—Horseman.

For some time after their first discovery these coins were attributed to Rezíah, and even now, assigned as they are to Ruckn ud din, there is much doubt as to their due appropriation: the best specimens, however, favor the reading now adopted, and show the ركن of Rukn pretty distinctly. There is a difficulty in the shape of the بن (bin), which looks more like بنت (binut); but the form of the coins and the tenor of the inscription differ so much from those of Rezíah, the only woman of our series, that these reasons alone would lead to a rejection of her claim to the money in dispute.

Sixth Reign (a.h. 634—637; a.d. 1236—1239).

Sultán Rezíah. This princess presents the remarkable incident in Mohammedan history of a reigning queen! Ferishtah, speaking of her, says, "there was no fault to be found with her but that she was a woman!" a most orthodox Mohammedan sneer, and one unfortunately too well justified in the present instance. Her capacity for business, and her sufficiency to fill and adorn a throne, had already been shown during the reign of her father, who, when absent from Delhi, had left her in charge of his government in preference to his sons. Nor did her early conduct after her elevation disappoint the fair expectations raised in her favor. The ability with which she dissolved the army of an opposing faction, even after its victory over her own forces, evinced aptitude in diplomacy of no mean order: her civil and judicial administration was equally admirably conducted: and, in short, she displayed all the qualities of an able and just sovereign. All her high endowments, all her achieved successes, were however destined to be sacrificed to a woman's weakness, which seems to have been reprobated more from the fact of the object of her attachment being of low degree (an Abyssinian slave) than from any supposed impropriety in the mere act of an empress loving. The objections taken by the nobles to her manifest partiality to this person were brought to a crisis by her elevating him to the dignity of Amír ul Amráh (chief of the nobles). Open revolt ensued, which resulted in the dethronement of the queen, who was made over for safe custody to Altunia, one of the leaders of the insurrection, and her brother, Behrám, raised to the musnud in her stead. Here again Rezíah displayed her subtilty in persuading Altunia to marry her, and then readily induced him to support her claims against his former confederates; which was so effectually done that it was not until after two severe battles that she was finally made prisoner and put to death.

27.—Silver. 165 grs. Unique. (*Prinsep Collection.*)

Obv.—السلطان الاعظم جلالة الدنيا و الدين ملكة ابنت التمش السلطان مهرة امير المومنين The most mighty Sultan, Jellálat ud dunia wa ud din (the glory of the world and the faith), the Queen, the daughter of the Sultan Altumsh, the beloved of the commander of the faithful.

℞.—Area - - في عهد الامام المستنصر امير المومنين
In the time of the Imám Al Mustunsir, the commander of the faithful.

Marg.— ستماية - - النضة

28 and 29.—Copper. 47 and 49 grs. V.R.

Obv.—السلطان الاعظم رضيه الد نيا و الدين The most mighty Sultan, Rezíah ud dunia wa ud din.

℞.—Horseman and Sri Hămīrăh.

Up to the present time the term *Rezíah* has been looked upon as implying a name and not a title; the coins above appear to demonstrate the contrary to be the fact: the silver medal negatively, inasmuch as it does not give *Rezíah* as a name; and the copper coins positively, in displaying the *Rezíah* joined to the *ud dunia*, &c. In a Persian MS. in the Library of the Royal Asiatic Society, denominated "Tarikhi Hind" (No. 125 of MS. Catalogue), she is also adverted to under the title of رضي الدين Rezí ud din, without any further attempt at designation. The meaning assigned to رضي is, *satisfying*. Her name may, therefore, be rendered, The approved.

It will be remarked that the coins retain the *Sultan* in the masculine gender, whereas all the rest of the Persian inscription is duly preserved in the feminine: this curious affectation of the superior sex in regard to her regal position, strongly supports the account of Ferishtah, that "changing her apparel" she "assumed the imperial robes."

SEVENTH KING (A.H. 637—639; A.D. 1239–1241).

The reign of Muaz ud din Behrám Sháh, in duration little more than two years, was marked during its continuance by the usual amount of intrigues, assassinations, and mutinies common to an Eastern court under a weak monarchy, and was finally brought to a close by the siege of the capital by the vizir, and the subsequent imprisonment and murder of the sovereign.

A partial invasion of the north of India, by the Moghuls of Zengiz Khán, took place during 639; they, however, penetrated no further than Lahore.

30 and 31.—Silver and Copper mixed. 54 and 56 grs. V.R.

Obv.—السلطان الاعظم معز الدنيا و الدين The most mighty Sultan, Muaz ud dunia wa ud din.

℞.—Horseman, and السلطان the Sultan.

32.—Silver and Copper mixed. Unique.

Obv.—सुलताण सा मुयजदीं Bull and Sultan Sā (Shah) Mūyăzădín.

℞.—श्री हमीरः Horseman and Sri Hămĭrăh.

Eighth King (A.H. 639—644; A.D. 1241—1246).

The uncertainty of succession to Eastern thrones is prominently displayed in the present instance, in the accession of two kings in one day. Eiz ud din Balbum, a son-in-law of Altumsh, supported by a faction, assumed the sovereignty immediately on the decease of Behrám; but, before night, he was supplanted by Alá ud din Masáud, a son of Rukn ud din Fírúz, upon whom the choice of the more influential nobles had fallen.

The reign of this prince was marked by the occurrence of two invasions of India by the Moghuls: in the one case, they penetrated through Thibet into Bengal, where they were met and defeated by the troops on the spot; in the other instance, their approach from the West was checked by the advance of the sultan in person. A two years' rule, otherwise remarkable only for the evil conduct of the sovereign, closed with his imprisonment and death.

A coin similar to No. 33, with the exception of the name of the khalif, which indicates an earlier date.

ª.—Copper. 169 grs. V.R.

R.—في عهد الامام المستنصر امير المومنين In the time of the Imám Al Mustansir, the commander of the faithful.

N.B. Al Mustansir died in 640 A.H.

33.—Silver. 168 grs. V.R.

Obv.—السلطان الاعظم علا الدنيا والدين ابو المظفر مسعود شاه بن السلطان The mighty King, Alá ud dunia wa ud din. The victorious Masáud Sháh, the son of the King.

Marg.— - - - سنه احدو - - ضرب

R.—Area - - في عهد الامام المستعصم امير المومنين -

In the time of the Imám Al Mustassem, the commander of the faithful.

Marg.—سنه احد و اربعين و ستمايه . . . Year 641.

34.—Silver and Copper. 50 grs.

Obv.—السلطان الاعظم علا الدنيا و الدين The mighty King, Alá ud dunia wa ud din.

R.—مسعود شاه Masáud Sháh.

35.—Copper. 49½ grs.

Obv.—الاعظم علا الدنيا و الدين مسعود شاه

R.—مسعودشاه

36.—Silver and Copper. 52 grs.

Obv.—مسعود بن سلطان ?

R.—Rude figure of a horseman.

37.—Copper. 56 grs.

Obv.—السلطان الاعظم مسعود السلطان

R.—Rude figure of a horseman.

38.—Copper and Silver. 41 grs.

Obv.—अलादिण Bull and Aládin.

NINTH KING (A.H. 644—663; A.D. 1246—1266).

The early part of the reign of Násir ud din Mahmúd has been rendered celebrated by the acts of his vizir, Balban; whose successful arrangements for the defence of the frontier from the attacks of the Moghuls (the crying evil of the day) were followed by measures equally efficient for the internal security and consolidation of the empire, by bringing under more perfect subjection many of the local Hindú rajahs, who had been enabled to disclaim their allegiance during the preceding reign. The jealousy of the sultan, consequent upon the great energy and influence of his vizir, led to the dismissal of the latter; but the somewhat authoritative demand of many of the provincial governors necessitated his speedy restoration. The exemplary private life of this monarch offers a strong contrast to the results usually attendant upon the power of unlimited indulgence incident to the occupation of an Asiatic throne.

39.—Silver. 170 grs. C.

Obv.—Area السلطان الاعظم ناصر الدنيا و الدين ابوالمظفر محمود ابن السلطان Date 688 H. The most mighty Sovereign Násir ud dunia wa ud din. The victorious Mahmúd, the son of the Sultan.

Both *Obv.* and *Rev. margin.*—ضرب هذه الفضة بحضرة دهلي في سنه ثمان خمسين و ستمايه This silver (coin was) struck at the capital, Delhí, in the year 658.

R.—Area - - في عهد الامام المستعصم امير المومنين In the time of the Imam Al Mostassem, the commander of the faithful.

40.—Silver and Copper. 51 grs.

Obv.—السلطان الاعظم ناصر الدنيا والدين The most mighty Sovereign Násir ud dunia wa ud din.

R.—श्री हमीरः محمود Mahmúd. Sri Hamírah.

41.—Copper. 54 grs.

Obv.—السلطان الاعظم ناصر الدنيا و الدين The most mighty Sovereign Násir ud dunia wa ud din.

Tenth King (A.H. 664—685; A.D. 1266—1286).

Mahmúd, leaving no male issue, the facile succession of his powerful vizir followed almost of necessity. Balban's conduct after his elevation was not altogether in accordance with the promise of his behaviour while a minister. Once a slave, now a king, the first endeavour of his reign was to destroy the very race of Túrkí bondmen among whom he himself had lately been numbered. In his own altered position, legitimacy was to become paramount. The inalienable succession of his own heirs was now to be secured. The contingency under which he had risen was, for the future, to be rendered impossible. To this end blood was not spared; and in this spirit the lives of his own near relations were sacrificed with but little compunction. The severity also which led to the wholesale depopulation of a province, albeit of bandits, attended by the slaughter of 100,000 human beings, was scarcely to be justified by a plea of far more urgent expediency than can be advanced in the instance in question. About this period, the disorder of the neighbouring kingdoms consequent upon the invasion of the Moghuls, drove the most illustrious men from all quarters to seek refuge in India. There, were assembled all the brightest ornaments of the Asiatic world; and, at their head, no less than fifteen sovereign princes. For a time, the old Hindú capital became, as it were, the centre of Mohammedanism; and Delhi shone with a splendour but little anticipated for it by its Moslim occupiers of a few short years before.

The unsparing rigour of the emperor secured his supremacy almost unquestioned throughout his long reign, with the exception of the one serious revolt of Tugrul, the governor of Bengal, who assumed the style and titles of an independent king, and was successful in defeating two several armies sent to subdue him. At length, the sultan proceeded against him in person, and coming upon the whole force of the rebels somewhat unexpectedly, he in a dashing spirit of chivalry, though at the head of only forty troopers, entered their camp at headlong speed, and struck panic into his adversaries by his very rashness. In the precipitate flight which ensued, Tugrul was captured and slain. Balban's loss of his eldest son, who fell in the hour of victory, fighting against the enemies of his race, the Moghuls, hastened the end for which, at the age of eighty, nature must already have prepared the way; and the emperor, in the language of his people, took the road to another world.

[b].—Gold. R. 169 grs. Date 678 H. (*Marsden.*)
Same type and legends as No. 42, with the exception of the word الذهب in place of الفضة

42.—Silver. 168 grs. R.
Obv.—السلطان الاعظم غياث الدنيا و الدين ابو المظفر بلبن السلطان The most mighty Sovereign, Ghiás ud dunia wa ud din. The victorious Balban, the Sultán.

R.—الامام المستعصم امير المومنين The Imám Al Mustassem, commander of the faithful.

Margin.—ضرب هذه الفضة بحضرة دهلي في سنه ثمان و سبعين و ستمايه This silver (coin was) struck at the capital, Delhí, in the year 678 H.

A change is to be noticed in the coins of Balban, in the rejection of the words *fí uhud*, "in the time of," "under the auspices of," usually prefixed to the name of the khalif on the medals of his predecessors. The last Abbasside khalif, Mustassem, was put to death in 656 A.H., by the Moghul conqueror of Baghdad, Hulaku Khan. It has been the subject of remark, as an apparent inconsistency, that Balban and other monarchs should have continued to employ the name of this martyr of their faith long subsequent to his decease; its retention, however, may be considered as appropriate, as it was clearly intentional; pending the appearance of an acknowledged successor to the throne of Mohammed, no course could have been less open to objection than a continuation of this simple record of the last who had borne the mantle of the Prophet.

43.—Copper. 47½ grs. C.

Obv.—السلطان الاعظم غياث الدنيا و الدين The most mighty Sovereign, Ghiás ud dunia wa ud din.

R.—*Centre* بلبن Balban. *Marg.* श्री: सुलतां गयास दीं Sri Sultán Ghiás ud din.

44.—Copper. 67 grs. C.

Obv.—السلطان الا عظم The most mighty Sovereign.

R.—غياث الدنيا و الدين Ghiás ud dunia wa ud din.

45.—Copper. 26 grs. V.R.

Obv.—عدل غياثى (The) just (coin of) Ghiás.

R.—حضرت دهلي At the capital, Delhí.

ELEVENTH KING (A.H. 685—687; A.D. 1286—1288).

Prior to the decease of his father, Bakarra Khan, then governor of Bengal, had been disinherited from the succession to the throne of Delhí, and Kaikhusrú, the son of his elder brother, Mohammed, had been nominated in his stead; but the nobles present in the capital at the time of the death of Balban superseded this last arrangement by elevating Kaikobád, another grandson of the emperor, and the son of Bakarra Khan himself. The governor of Bengal, on receiving information of the state of matters at Delhí, marched towards that metropolis for the purpose of asserting his own right to the crown; but being met on the way by the army of his son, he returned to Bengal without any further effort, leaving Kaikobád the now undisputed monarch of Hindústán. The early part of this reign, conspicuous for the dissipation of the king, and the influence and oppressive conduct of the vizir, was marked by the foul and needless massacre of the Moghul mercenaries in the service of the state. The emperor's father, who had retained the kingdom of Bengal, hearing of the position of thraldom to which his son was reduced, by the domination of his vizir, endeavoured to remedy the evil by warnings. Seeing these of no effect, he moved an army towards the capital. The son was not slow to meet him, and the two forces encamped nearly in sight of each other. But Bakarra Khan, or, as he had been called since the death of Balban, Násir ud din, finding himself inferior to the troops opposed to him, and being unwilling to leave his son, as of old, in the power of his minister, desired an interview, with the object of endeavouring, by personal persuasion, to effect what written remonstrances had failed to accomplish.

Under the advice of the vizir an audience was conceded, but only on terms of the most abject humiliation possible for the father. When, however, these came to be carried out, and the meeting between father and son actually took place, in the presence of the whole court, the supremacy of nature had its way, and the son would now have humbled himself even as he had been taught to humiliate his sire.

The meeting ended in a recognition of the independence of the kingdom of Bengal, but was useless for the purpose for which it had been sought. The murder of the minister, in 688, but little improved the now paralytic king's position; he was only surrounded by new intriguers for power, the competition for which ended in favour of Fírúz Khiljí, whose last step to the foot of the throne was over the corpse of his predecessor; the small remains of whose life left little to be done by his assassins.

46.—Silver. 168 grs. R.

Obv.—السلطان الاعظم معز الدنيا و الدين ابو المظفر كيقباد السلطان Date, 687. The most mighty Sovereign, Muaz ud dunia wa ud din. The victorious Kaikobád, the Sultan.

R.—الامام المستعصم امير الموءمنين The Imám Al Mustassem, commander of the faithful.

Marg.—ضرب هذه الفضة بحضرت دهلي في سنه سبع و ثمانين و ستمايه This silver (coin was) struck at the capital, Delhí, in the year 687.

47.—Silver and Copper. 54 grs.

Obv.—السلطان الاعظم معز الدنيا و الدين The most mighty Sovereign, Muaz ud dunia wa ud din.

R.—كيقباد Kaikobád. श्री सुलतां मुःजुदीं Sri Sultán Mu-ujudin.

This word presents a curious instance of the difficulty of expressing the sounds of certain letters of the Arabic alphabet in the written Hindí language. There being no consonant corresponding with the Arabic ع as used in معز the die-cutter, not satisfied with the मुयजदीं of his predecessors, has apparently invented a letter for the occasion, composed of the final visarga (:) placed horizontally; to which has been attached the vowel ُ ŭ; making the whole something like Mu-*oh*ujudin.

48.—Copper. 51 grs.

Obv.—السلطان الاعظم The most mighty Sovereign,

R.—معز الدنيا و الدين Muaz ud dunia wa ud din.

49.—Copper. 59 grs.

Obv.—عدل معزي The just (coin of) Muaz.

R.—بحضرت دهلي. The capital, Delhí.

TWELFTH KING (A.H. 687—695; A.D. 1288—1295).

Fírúz's accession does not appear to have been immediate on the death of the late king, as native historians mention the succession of Shums ud din Kai Kaus, a son of Kaikobád,[8] who is said to have reigned for three months and some days. Ferishtah also, though he does not allow him a separate reign, indirectly countenances the fact, in his notice of the murder of this prince by Fírúz, as an early act towards the consolidation of his own power.

The seven years' domination over the destinies of Hindústán of this, the first of the race of Khiljí, notable, in as far as the sovereign was concerned, only for his unwise clemency, has been rendered remarkable by the extensive campaigns of his nephew, Alá ud din; whose expedition into the Dekhin—as successful as it was daring—was the means of securing for this leader the enormous wealth which enabled him first to rebel, and eventually to possess himself of the crown of Delhí. Intrigue, however, was found more suitable than overt insurrection; and, in a moment of unwise confidence, Fírúz ventured with but a slight

---

[8] See Aíen i Akhberí and Mirát al Alem, &c.

escort into the camp of his deceiver, where he was assassinated under circumstances of more than usual atrocity.

50.—Silver. 168 grs. R.

Obv.—السلطان الاعظم جلال الدنيا و الدين ابو المظفر فيروز شاه السلطان The most mighty Sovereign, Jelal ud dunia wa ud din. The victorious Fírúz Sháh, the Sultan.

R.—Area الامام المستعصم امير المومنين

The Imám Al Mustassem, commander of the faithful.

Marg.—ضرب هذه الفضة بحضرة دهلي في سنه خمس و تسعين و ستمايه This silver (coin was) struck at the capital, Delhí, in the year 695.

51.—Silver. 52 grs.

Obv.—السلطان الاعظم جلال الدنيا و الدين The most mighty Sovereign, Jelal ud dunia wa ud din.

R.—*Centre* فيروز شاه Fírúz Sháh.

Marg.—श्री: सुलतां जलालुदीं Sri Sultán Jalaludin.

52.—Copper. 67 grs.

Obv.—السلطان الاعظم The most mighty Sovereign,

R.—جلال الدنيا و الدين Jelal ud dunia wa ud din.

53.—Copper. 29 grs.

Obv.—عدل فيروز شاه Just (coin of) Fírúz Sháh.

R.—بحضرت دهلي At the capital, Delhí.

There are certain coins similar in character to Nos. 16, 32, and 41, bearing the legend सा जलालदिं which probably should be attributed to this sultan; but in the absence of any means of identification beyond the mere title, and adverting to the apparent discontinuance of the use of this species of coin at this period, there may be some doubt as to the possibility of the specimens in question belonging either to Rezíah or Jelál ud din Khárizm Sháh; who, it is to be remarked, held sovereignty in the Punjab, for a short time, during the reign of Altumsh.

THIRTEENTH KING (A.H. 695; A.D. 1295).

On the murder of his father, in the camp of Alá ud din, Rukn ud din Ibrahím was elevated to the throne of Hindústán. His party being in possession of the capital, gave him a temporary existence as a king—a dignity which otherwise, as a younger son and a minor, he was neither entitled nor fitted to hold. Alá ud din, having already at his command a powerful army, and the booty of the Duckhun supplying him with means of increasing his force to an almost unlimited extent, had merely to advance to Delhí to put an end to the rule of the boy king, whose safety was for a time secured by a precipitate flight to Multán.

54.—Silver. 167 grs. Unique. (*Lord Auckland's Cabinet.*)

Obv.—السلطان الاعظم ركن الدنيا و الدين ابو المظفر ابرهيم شاه السلطان بن The most mighty Sovereign, Rukn ud dunia wa ud din. The victorious Ibrahím Sháh, the Sultán, son of—

R.—السلطان الاعظم جلال الدنيا و الدين فيروز شاه ناصر امير المومنين The most mighty Sultán, Jelal ud dunia wa ud din, Fírúz Sháh, supporter of the commander of the faithful.

Marg.—ضرب هذا الفضة بحضرت دهلي سنه خمس و تسعين و ستمايه This silver (coin was) struck in the capital, Delhí, in the year 695.

55.—Copper. 52 grs. R.

Obv.—السّطان الاعظم ركن الدنيا و الدين The most mighty Sovereign, Rukn ud dunia wa ud din.

R.—ابرهيم شاه بن فيروز شاه Ibrahím Sháh, son of Fírúz Sháh.

56.—Copper. 38 grs. R.

Obv.—عدل ابرهيم شاه Just (coin of) Ibrahím Sháh,

R.—بن فيروز شاه son of Fírúz Sháh.

FOURTEENTH KING (A.H. 695—716; A.D. 1295—1316).

Alá ud din Mohammed Sháh, the most energetic and powerful of the Moslim monarchs who had yet swayed the destinies of Hindústán, consolidated his authority after his accession by means as little scrupulous as those which he had used in its attainment. His own individual efforts to this end were aided by the successes of his generals against the last remaining stronghold of the family of Fírúz in Multán, the repulse of a Moghul invasion in the Punjab, and the reduction of the kingdom of Guzrát. In 698 A.H., Northern India was desolated by another invasion of the Moghuls: this time, the expedition being conducted with skill, and supported by an overwhelming force, the assailants met with but little effectual opposition till they reached the gates of Delhí. Here, under the walls of his capital, the sultan was forced to give them battle: "two such mighty hosts had not before been arrayed against each other since the day when the spears of Islám were first exalted in Hindústán.' The conflict was not of long duration, and victory declared itself in favor of the arms of Alá ud din. The activity of the pursuit gave a lesson to the invaders which sufficed for the time to carry them well out of the country they had looked upon as already conquered.

"In the third year of Alá ud din, when prosperity shone upon his arms, he began to form some extraordinary projects. One of these was the formation of a new system of religion, that, like Mohammed, he might be held in veneration by posterity. His other design was equally romantic. He proposed to leave a viceroy in India, and, like the great Alexander, to undertake the conquest of the world. In consequence of this project, he assumed the title of سكندر الثاني *Sekunder al Sání*, Alexander the Second, which was struck upon the currency of the empire."[9] Fortunately for the sultan, these crude schemes were submitted for approval to one of his subjects, who was bold enough to point out their absurdity even in the presence of the despot who had originated them. Thus the monarch's eccentricities resulted in no worse consequences than the assumption of certain ridiculous titles still to be seen on his coinage;[10] indeed, the opportune truths told on this occasion, as to what he had yet to accomplish in the immediate circle of his own dominions, led to the confirmation and extension of his already immense power.

A conspiracy, attended by an attempt at assassination, from which the sultan escaped almost by a miracle, was followed by an insurrection as singular in many of its circumstances. During his absence from his capital, a revolution was accomplished, which actually placed a new sovereign on the throne. A seven days' reign was, however, all that was accorded to the new monarch, and his life and the lives of not a few who had aided his temporary elevation, paid the penalty of their rashness.

Again, a third time, an inroad of the Moghuls threatened the most serious results. The sultan, unable to meet his

[9] Dow's Ferishtah, vol. i., page 234.
[10] Vide Nos. 57 and 58.

adversaries in the open field, allowed himself to be besieged in his own capital; once more, however, fortune favoured him, and the Moghuls returned as they came.

Towards the latter part of this reign, the conquests of the eunuch Káfur, who commanded the army of the Dukhun, enabled him to bring to Delhí the plunder acquired during his various expeditions, to the almost unheard-of extent of 96,000 maunds of gold alone, independent of spoil of other descriptions to a proportionate amount.

Of Alá ud din's riches, generally, it is related that his wealth surpassed the accumulations of the ten campaigns of Mahmúd of Ghazní. The closing scene of this monarch's life was now approaching, and his last moments of pain and debasement were rendered utterly unendurable to his proud spirit by the repeated reports of insurrections which began to rise up on all sides. The 16th of Shaval, 716 A.H., witnessed the last moments of this mighty king.

It is remarkable, that the existing money of this prince should so directly bear out the relation of historians as to his enormous wealth. Both his silver and gold coins are found to this day in the greatest abundance; but the amount of his gold coinage which is extant, is peculiarly noticeable as regarding its relative proportion to the same species of money of his predecessors, whose gold coins are so rare as to be, with one exception, almost unknown.

°.—Gold. 170 grs. C.

Type and legend identical with No. 57 silver coin, with the exception of the word السكه taking the place of الفضة

57.—Silver. 170 grs. C.

Obv.—السلطان الاعظم علا الدنيا و الدين ابو المظفر محمد شاه السلطان The most mighty sovereign, Alá ud dunia wa ud din, Abúl Muzafar, Mohammed Sháh, the Sultan.

R.—*Area* سكندر الثاني يمين الخلافة ناصر امير المومنين
Sekunder the second, right hand of the khalifat, supporter of the commander of the faithful.

Marg.—ضرب هذه الفضة بحضرت دهلي في سنه اثني عشر و سبعمايه, This silver (was) struck at the capital, Delhí, in the year 712.

58.—Copper and Silver.

Obv.—علا الدنيا و الدين سكندر الثاني

R.—Horseman, similar to No. 32.

59.—Silver and Copper. 55 grs. Date 702.

Obv.—السلطان الا عظم علا الدنيا و الدين

R.—ابو المظفر محمد شاه السلطان ٧٠٢

60.—Copper. 55 grs. Date 710.

Obv.—السلطان الا عظم علا الدنيا و الدين

R.—*Area* محمد شاه

Marg. श्री सलतां अलावदीं ७१०

The coins, Nos. 59 and 60, are remarkable as offering the first instance in the present series of the general use of numerals in recording dates; it having been hitherto the custom to write the numbers in the full length of their respective Arabic denominations.

61.—Copper. 67 grs.

Obv.—السلطان الا عظم

R.—علا الدنيا و الدين

62.—Copper. 23 grs.

Obv.—عدل محمد شاه

R—بحضرت دهلي.

In concluding this reference to the coins of Alá ud din,

it may not be inappropriate to append the following note from Ferishtah, on the currency of this particular period.

"In order to comprehend the true value of the money of that day, it is proper to state that a tunka was equal to a tola in weight (180 grs.), whether of gold or silver; and a tunka of silver was equal to 50 jetuls. The jetul was a small copper coin, the weight of which is not now known: some conceive it was a tola, while others are of opinion that the jetul, like the pice of the present day, weighed $\frac{3}{4}$ tola. The maund of the time of Jellál ud din (Fírúz) weighed 40 seers, and each seer weighed 24 tolas."—*Ferishtah.* See Briggs, vol. i., page 361.

The following coin, in its date and near approximation in type to those of the Delhí series, claims notice in this place. Owing, however, to the absence of distinct historical information regarding any individual, who, about this period, obtained the title of Shums ud din Fírúz, as well as from the erasure of the place of mintage of the coin itself, no satisfactory attribution can well be attempted; at the same time, it may be suggested as possibly the production of the temporary king of the city of Delhí, who for seven days occupied the throne of his master, whose name was Alawi, or Sháh Nunní, but whose regal titles are unknown; or, it may belong to a Bengal mint, as the tenor of the inscription on the reverse is unlike that employed by Alá ud din himself, and assimilates closely to the form found in use, immediately subsequent to this epoch, on the coins of Ghiás ud din Bahádur Sháh, of Bengal.[11]

---

[11] The subjoined extract from the "Travels of Ibn Batuta," though in itself insufficient to justify a final conclusion on the subject, gives weight to the second conjecture now advanced, in affording in part a name similar to that recorded on the unattributed piece, in immediate connexion with the country to which the coin itself seems referable. This is not the place to attempt to reconcile the conflicting statements of the various authors whose evidence is available, nor is the subject matter of the enquiry

Silver. 165 grs.

Obv.—السّلطان الاعظم شمس الدنيا و الدين ابو المظفر فيروز شاه السلطان The most mighty sovereign, Shums ud dunia wa ud din, Abúl Muzafar Fírúz Sháh, the Sultan.

℞.—الامام المستعصم امير المومنين The Imam Al Mostassem, commander of the faithful.

Marg.—ضرب هذه الفضه بحضرت - - في سنه اثني و سبعمايه This silver (was) struck at the capital, (?) in the year 702.

FIFTEENTH KING (A.H. 616—617; A.D. 1316—1317).

On the demise of Alá ud din, Káfur, who had long possessed all real power in the state, set aside the more

---

sufficiently important in its relation to the numismatic history of the kings of Delhí to justify a lengthened examination of the whole question; it is however to be noticed, that Ibn Batuta's statement, in spite of its being that of a contemporary, is open to considerable doubt, as the detail is somewhat inexplicable in itself. It is affirmed by this author (page 116), that Násir ud din, the known governor of Bengal and son of Balban, died in 689; in the following quotation it will be seen that this same governor of Bengal and son of Balban is apparently represented as still living, but is now entitled *Shums ud din.* One of two inferences is here inevitable: either that Ferishtah and others, who extend the life of Násir ud din to the reign of Tuglak, have made two persons into one, or that Ibn Batuta has made one into two; at the same time, it is by no means improbable that one individual may have been known by two different titles.

"The father himself (Ghiás ud din Tuglak) then undertook an expedition against the province of Luknouti, in which resided at that time the sultan, Shams od din, son of Ghiáth od din Balaban: to whom had fled the Emírs of Toglik, as just mentioned. About this time, however, Shams od din died, having first bound his son, Shahab od din (by contract), who accordingly took possession of the throne; his younger brother, however, Ghiáth od din Bahádur Búrah, overcame him, and seized upon the kingdom."—*Dr. Lee's "Ibn Batuta,"* page 128.

mature sons of the late monarch to make way for Umur Khan, a boy of seven years of age, Káfur himself assuming the office of regent. But little time was allowed to elapse before two of the brothers of the nominal sovereign were deprived of sight, and the life of the third, Mubárik, attempted by the agents of the regent. This prince, however, having found means to buy off his executioners, was in his turn raised to supremacy by the death of Káfur, who was killed by the officers of the foot guard, within thirty-five days of his attainment of the office he so little deserved. Mubárik, it is said, did not assume the title of king until two months subsequent to this event, when his younger brother, in the loss of his eyes, met the fate usually accorded to those scions of the royal blood whom it was desirable to incapacitate from reigning, but whose bare life it was thought advisable to spare.

63.—Silver and Copper. 54½ grs. Unique.

Obv.—السلطان الا عظم شهاب الدنيا و الدين The most mighty sovereign, Shaháb ud dunia wa ud din.

R.—٧١٦ ابو المظفر عمر شاه السلطان Abul Muzafar Umur Sháh, the Sultan. 716.

Marsden adverts to three or four specimens of a silver coin in the museum of the East India Company, bearing the title of شهاب الدين which he considers as possibly belonging to Shaháb ud din Umur: these coins are not at present to be found. This, however, is the less a matter of regret, as far as the present series is concerned; as, from the tenor of what Marsden has been able to decipher, there is great reason to doubt the accuracy of the attribution suggested, and to suppose that the coins in question must have been the produce of some Bengal mint of a somewhat later period.

SIXTEENTH KING (A.H. 717—721; A.D. 1317—1321).

Mubárik, on proclaiming himself king, seemed determined that the means by which he had been elevated should no longer exist to be used against himself; with this intent, the officers who had assisted in the assassination of Káfur were put to death; and, at the same time, the guard, hitherto under their command, was broken up. Among many other slaves raised to offices of high rank by the new monarch, one Khusrú Khán, a converted Hindú, who was invested with the office of vizir, is noticeable, as having subsequently played a prominent part in the history of the day.

Some of the early actions of Mubárik are mentioned with commendation; but after little more than a twelve months' reign, his real disposition began to display itself in acts of the most unbridled licentiousness.

The favourite Khusrú being appointed to the command of the army in the Dukhun, and being successful in the conquest of Malabar, returned to the capital loaded with plunder; and, at this time, the sultan's habits having well prepared him to receive a master, Khusru made ready use of the position in which he found himself, and on the 25th of Rubbí ul Awul (third month), of 721 H., succeeded in accomplishing the destruction of his sovereign.

[d].—Gold. 165 grs. Similar to No. 65. Date wanting. (*Prinsep Cabinet.*)[11]

64.—Silver. 170 grs. V.R.

Obv.—السّلطان الا عظم قطب الدنيا و الدين ابو المظفر مبارک شاه السلطان بن السّلطان The most mighty sovereign,

[11] See also Fraehn, Num. Kufi. ex var. Museis selecti, Petropoli, A.D. 1823, page 80.

Kutb ud dunia wa ud din Abúl Muzafar Mubárik Sháh, the Sultan, son of the Sultan.

R.—*Area* اسکندر الزمان يمين الخلافة ناصر امير المومنين Alexander of the age, right hand of the khalifat, supporter of the commander of the faithful.

Marg.—ضرب هذه الفضة بحضرة دهلي في سنه سبع عشر و سبعمايه This silver (was) struck at the capital, Delhi, in the year 717.

65.—Silver. 169 grs. V.R. Square.

Obv.—الامام الا عظم خليفه ربّ العالمين قطب الدنيا و الدين ابو المظفر مبارکشاه The most mighty Imám, Khalif lord of the universe, Kutb ud dunia wa ud din, Abúl Muzafar Mubárik Sháh—

R.—*Area* السّلطان ابن السّلطان الواثق باللّه امير المومنين the Sultan, son of the Sultan, Al Wásik Billah, commander of the faithful.

Marg.—ضرب هذه السّكه بحضرة دارالخلافة في سنه ثمان عشر وسبعمايه This coin (was) struck at the capital, the seat of the khalifat, in the year 718.

Whatever Alá ud din's designs in regard to new systems of religion may have amounted to, it remained to his son to disavow entirely the spiritual supremacy of all other khalifs and successors of khalifs, and to appropriate that title to himself. This is evidenced in coin No. 65, which displays a simultaneous change from the comparatively humble epithet of "Right hand of the khalifat," &c., in conjunction with the marginal record of "struck at the capital, Delhí," to be found on the early coinage of the reign, to the style and title of "The most mighty Imám," as a prefix to Mubárik's self-assumed sacerdotal designation of Al Wásik Billah, accompanied by a marginal legend, showing that

Delhí in this change had arrived at the honors of a second Bagdhad.[12]

66.—Copper and Silver. 55 grs. Date 716.

Obv.—السلطان الاعظم قطب الدنيا و الدين

R.—مبارکشاه السلطان بن السلطان ٧١٦

The date on this coin of 716 A.H., would seem to show that the time fixed by Ferishtah for Mubárik's accession, viz. the 7th Muhurum, or the first Arabic month of 717, is incorrect.[13] It is probable, however, that the author in question may have adopted the day of the incarceration of Umur, and the public avowal of his supercession by the new sovereign, as the proper date of the commencement of the reign, in preference to, or in ignorance of, the exact period when supreme power was first assumed by Mubárik.

67.—Copper and Silver. 55 grs. Date 717.

Obv.—الامام الاعظم قطب الدنيا و الدين ٧١٧

R.—ابو المظفر مبارکشاه السلطان بن السلطان

68.—Copper and Silver. 55 grs.

Obv.—خليفه ربّ العالمين قطب الدنيا و الدين ابو المظفر ٧١٧

R.—مبارکشاه السلطان ابن السلطان الواثق بالله امير المومنين

---

[12] The following inscription, taken from a leaden cast of a coin in the Prinsep collection, shows that this mutation took place in the year 717.

Silver. Round. 717 H.

Obv.—الامام الاعظم قطب الدنيا و الدين ابو المظفر خليفه الله

R.—مبارکشاه السّلطان ابن السّلطان الواثق بالله امير المو-منين

Marg.—ضرب هذه الفضة بحضرة دارالخلافة في سنه سبع عشر و سبعمايه

[13] Dow's Ferishtah, vol. i., page 265.

69.—Silver. 55 grs. Square. Date 718.

Obv.—Margin خليفه الله ابو المظفر

Square area قطب الدنيا و الدين

R.—٧١٨ مبارکشاه السلطان ابن السلطان

70.—Copper and Silver. 56 grs. Square. Date 720.

Obv.—Same legend as No. 67.

R.—٧٢٠ خليفه الله مبارکشاه السلطان ابن السلطان

71.—Copper. Square. 66 grs.

Obv.—الامام الا عظم

R.—قطب الدنيا و الدين

72.—Copper. Square. 33 grs.

Obv.—عدل مبارکشاه

R.—بحضرة دارالخلافة

In terminating this notice of the money of Mubárik, it is requisite to make a passing allusion to certain coins of Behádur Sháh, both in reference to the temporary severance of the eastern portion of the kingdom of Bengal from the empire of Hindustan, as well as in the hope of elucidating the enquiry into the due identification of a piece but little dissimilar in its general style and reverse legend, a description of which is given in the note appended to the detail of the coins of Alá ud din. The following extract from Stewart's History of Bengal sufficiently explains the circumstances under which this governor first began to coin money:—

"The emperor (Alá ud din) at the same time appointed a chief, named Behádur Khan, to the government of the eastern districts of Bengal; hoping, by thus dividing that province into two governments, to render it more subservient to the court of Delhí than it had hitherto proved. The capital of the new government was fixed at Sunergong.[13]

"But, in the year 717 H., when the dissolute prince, Mubárik Sháh, succeeded to the throne of Delhí, Behádur, despising the weakness of the imperial councils, arrogated to himself independence; assuming the white umbrella, and ordering the coin to be stamped with his own name, changing the title of Behádur Khan to Behádur Sháh."—*Stewart's Bengal*, page 79.

The newly erected kingdom thus created did not exist for any considerable period, but was re-attached to Delhí in the reign of Ghiás ud din Tuglák.

These coins are by no means uncommon, but are of inferior workmanship, and generally in imperfect preservation; so much so, that of the five or six specimens at present available for reference, the following legend is the most complete attainable.

Silver. 169 grs.

Obv.—السّلطان الا عظم غياث الدنيا و الدين ابو المظفر بهادر شاه السلطان بن ک - - -

℞.—*Area* الامام المستعصم امير المومنين

Marg. ضرب هذه الفضة بحضرت - في سنه احدي عشرين و سبعمايه

SEVENTEENTH KING (A.H. 721, RUBBI UL AWUL; A.D. 1321).

Having succeeded in ridding himself of the single obstacle to his own advance to supremacy, Khusrú proclaimed himself sultan under the title of Násir ud din, and endeavoured to strengthen his hold on the rank he had assumed by the massacre of all the survivors of the family of Alá ud din.

[13] Thirteen miles south-east from Dacca.

He, at the same time, attempted to attach the nobles of the court to his person by loading them with the titles and dignities at his command. This system availed only for a time; and the governor of the Punjáb, advancing with the forces of that province, put an end to the usurpation which had endured somewhat less than five months.

73.—Silver. Unique. (*Original in possession of Col. Stacy.*)

Obv.—السلطان الا عظم ناصر الدنيا و الدين ابو المظفر

The most mighty Sultan, Násir ud dunia wa ud din Abúl Muzafar.

R.—خسرو شاه السلطان الواثق خير الرحمن ولي امير المومنين Khusrú Sháh, the Sultan Al Wásik Khair al Rehman (relying upon the goodness of the All-merciful), successor to the commander of the faithful.

Marg.—ضرب هذه الف - - - عشرين و سبعمايه

74.—Copper. (*Lord Auckland.*)

Obv.—السلطان الا عظم ناصر الدنيا و الدين ٠(٧٢)

R.—*Centre* خسرو شاه

Marg.—السلطان ولي امير المومنين

The only numeral visible on this coin is that which must of necessity be taken to be the final figure of the annual date. This particular figure, looking to the then uncertain method of formation, as noticeable on the coins of the Patán kings immediately antecedent to the reign to which this piece refers, may either be taken to represent a naught or a five.[14] Accepting then the nearest proximate date, concluding with either one or the other of these numerals, it will be necessary to refer the issue of this coin to either the year 720 or 725: as the sultan whose name it bears is stated by historians to have attained power on the 25th

[14] Ex. gr. see coins 59 and 79.

of the third month of 721 H. The former is naturally the preferable date: in adopting it, but slight violence is done to the probably accumulated errors of successive MS. copyists, who have each in their day transcribed the history of Hindústán from the 14th to the 19th century.

EIGHTEENTH KING (A.H. 721—725; A.D. 1321—1325).

On the 1st of Shabán, 721, Gházi Beg Tuglak, the governor of Lahore, who had relieved Delhí from the rule of Khusrú, entered the capital in triumph, and, appealing to the people to choose their own sovereign, he was himself elected by acclamation, receiving from the populace the title of *Sháh Jehán* (king of the world); which epithet, however, he replaced by the more modest denomination of *Ghiás ud din* (defender of the faith). The early arrangements for the peace and security of his dominions adopted by the monarch thus elevated, fully justified the selection of the citizens of the metropolis.

The second year of this reign was marked by the failure of the army under Fukur ud din Júnah, the heir apparent, in an attempt to take Wurangól: to this succeeded a somewhat calamitous retreat, which ended in the prince's reaching Delhí with but a small remnant of the host by whom he had once been supported. Little time, however, was allowed to elapse before a more determined and better organised effort against this place met with full success.

In 724, the emperor proceeded in person into Bengal: here he received the allegiance of Násir ud din, the son of the sultan Balban; who, from the date of his first appointment in 680 H., had, under various terms and with varied boundaries, held the dependencies of this government, and who had already outlived no less than eight of the sultans who had in turn attained the throne of Delhí. He was now again confirmed in the charge of Western Bengal, Tatar Khan, the sultan's adopted son, being entrusted with the direction of the eastern portion of that kingdom, where he succeeded in defeating and capturing the rebel governor, Buhádur Sháh. Ghias ud din, on his return to Hindústán, was met by his son Júnah, who had been left as his representative in Delhí. During the course of an entertainment, given in honor of the occasion, the emperor was killed by the fall of a portion of a temporary building, which had been hastily erected to receive him.

75.—Gold. 171 grs. V.R.

Obv.—السّلطان السعيد الشهيد الغازي غياث الدنيا و الدين

The sultan, the fortunate, the testifier, the Ghází, Ghiás ud dunia wa ud din.

R.—*Area* ابو المظفر تغلقشاه انار اللّه برهانه ۷۲۱ Abúl Muzafar Tughlak Sháh. May God illumine his testimony. 721.

Marg.—ضرب هذه السكه - - عشرين و سبعمايه

This coin was struck - - (in) seven hundred and twenty- . .

76.—Gold. 173 grs. R.

Obv.—السّطان الغازي غياث الدنيا و الدين ابو المظفر The sultan, the Ghází, Ghiás ud dunia wa ud din Abúl Muzafar.

R.—*Area* سكندر الثاني يمين الخلافة ناصر امير المومنين

Alexander the Second, right hand of the khalifat, supporter of the commander of the faithful.

Marg.— - - صزب هذه اا

77.—Silver. 170 grs. R.

Obv.—السّلطان الغازي غياث الدنيا و الدين ابو المظفر

R.—*Area* تغلق شاه السّلطان ناصر امير المومنين

Marg.—ضرب هذه السكه بقلعة ديوگير في سنه احدي عشرين و سبعمايه, This coin (was) struck at the fortress of Deogír, in the year 721.

78.—Silver. 170 grs. R. A similar coin struck at Delhí in 724.

R.—*Marg.* ضرب هذه السكه بحضرة دهلي في سنه اربع و عشرين و سبعمايه

79.—Silver and copper. 54 grs.

Obv.—٧٢٥ السّطان الغازي غياث الدنيا و الدين

R.—*Area* تغلق شاه

Marg.—श्रीः सुलतां गयासुदीं

80.—Silver and copper. 55 grs. C.

Obv.—السّلطان الغازي غياث الدنيا و الدين

R.—٧٢١ ابو المظفر تغلق شاه السّلطان

81.—Copper. 53 grs. R.

Obv.—تغلق

R.—شاة

NINETEENTH KING (A.H. 725—752; A.D. 1325—1351).

On the death of his father, Fukur ud din Júnah, otherwise called Aluf Khán, ascended the throne of Delhí under the title of Mohammed bin Tuglak. The epoch of this accession has been rendered notable by the immense sums which were lavished by the new monarch with almost unexampled profusion. Mohammed Tuglak's personal acquirements are described by the writers of the day in the most laudatory terms: he was, at the same time, the most eloquent and accomplished prince of his time; his letters, both in Persian and Arabic, have been since regarded as models of such compositions: in brief, he was "one of the wonders of the age in which he lived." The only failing he was as yet discovered to possess, was "a want of mercy." In 727, Hindústán was invaded by the Moghul Turmushrín Khán: the emperor, unable to oppose him, was forced to buy off the Gaul with almost the price of the kingdom he wished to save. About this time, Mohammed Tuglak turned his attention to the reduction of the countries to the southward of his own dominions, and succeeded so effectually, that many valuable provinces were as fully "incorporated with the empire as the villages in the vicinity of Delhí:" he also subdued the whole Carnatic to the extremities of the Dukhun, from sea to sea; but, in the convulsions which shortly afterwards shook the kingdom, all these new acquisitions, with the single exception of Guzrát, were again lost. The principal causes of the disturbances here alluded to, were, the heavy taxes, the issue of copper money as the representative of silver, and the enrolment of the enormous armies which the emperor's schemes of conquest rendered necessary. The year 738 witnessed the first preparatory expedition towards the visionary project of his conquest of China: in the history of the same year is to be recorded the fact, that of the 100,000 men despatched upon this insensate attempt, scarcely a man returned to Delhí. Shortly after this, his still more infatuated design of removing the capital and its denizens from Delhí to Deogir, took possession of the sultan's mind: men, women and children, with all belonging to them, were to be transported to the new metropolis; trees, even, were to be made subject to the will of the despot, and, torn up by their roots and replanted on the road to the new capital, they were to furnish shade to the wayfarers who were destined to compose the population of the king-created city. Absolute force seems to have prevailed: its effects, however, were but transitory; for, at the end of two years, it was found necessary to renew this strange transportation; and Delhí, the much-loved home of many, was once again left desolate.[14] In fit keeping with these mad acts, was the absolute hunting of human beings, recorded against this monarch.

With the exception of the erection of an independent Mohammedan state in the Dukhun under Hussun Gungó (the foundation of the subsequently powerful dynasty of the Bahmaní kings of Kalbarga), the still varied tenor of the remaining eleven years of Mohammed Tuglak's domination does not offer any points of sufficient prominence to claim record in these brief notes.

82.—Gold. 200 grs. R.

Obv.—اشهد ان لا اله الا الله و اشهد ان محمدا عبده و رسوله
I bear witness that there is no god but God, and I testify that Mohammed is his servant and apostle.

℞.—*Area* الواثق بتائيد الرحمن محمد شاه السلطان
The confiding in the benignity of the Merciful, Mohammed Shah, the sultan.

Marg.—ضرب هذا الدينار بحضرة دهلي سنه ست و عشرين و سبعمايه This dínár was struck at the capital, Delhí, (in the) year 726.

---

[14] The following account of Ibn Batuta, who was in part an eye-witness of the transactions referred to, will give some idea of the horrors perpetrated in carrying out this edict:—

"Upon this they all went out; but his servants finding a blind man in one of the houses, and a bed-ridden one in another, the emperor commanded the bed-ridden man to be projected from a balista (في المنجنيق), and the blind one to be dragged by his feet to Dawlatabad, which is at the distance of ten days, and he was so dragged; but his limbs dropping off by the way, only one of his legs was brought to the place intended, and was then thrown into it: for the order had been that they should go to this place. When I entered Delhí it was almost a desert."

83.—Gold. 137 grs. V.R.

Obv.—ضرب في زمن العبد الراجي رحمة الله محمد بن تغلق Struck in the time of the servant, trusting in the mercy of God, Mohammed son of Tughlak.

R.—*Centre* لا اله الا الله محمد رسول الله There is no god but God, Mohammed is the apostle of God.

Marg.—هذا الدينار بحضرة دهلي في سنه سبع و عشرين و سبعمايه This dínár, at the capital, Delhí, in the year 727.

84.—Gold. 171 grs. R.

Obv.—والله الغني وانتم الفقرا God is the rich, and ye (are) the poor.

R.—*Centre* في عهد محمد بن تغلق In the reign of Mohammed, son of Tughlak.

Marg.—بحضرة دهلي سنه ست و ثلثين و سبعمايه At the capital, Delhí, year 736

85.—Gold. 167 grs. R.

Obv.—ضرب هذا الدينار الخليفتي الدهلي في شهور سنه اثني و اربعي (اربعين) وسبعمايه This dínár of the Delhí khalifat was struck in the months of the year 742.

R.—في زمان الامام المستكفي بالله امير المومنين ابو الربيع سليمان خلد الله خلافته In the time of the Imám, Al Mostakfi Billah, commander of the faithful, Abúl Rubí Sulímán, may God perpetuate his khalifat.

86.—Gold. 171 grs. R.

Obv.—في زمان الامام امير المومنين الحاكم بامر In the time of the Imám, commander of the faithful, Al Hakim Beamur.

R.—الله ابو العباس احمد خلد ملكه Illahi Abúl Abbás Ahmud, may his reign endure.

The subjoined extract gives the details of Mohammed Tuglak's doubts and difficulties, arising out of the want of due sacerdotal confirmation of the title by which he held his throne.

A.H. 743. "The king, at this time, took it into his head that all the calamities of his reign proceeded from his not having been confirmed on his throne by the Abassy Caliph. He, therefore, despatched presents and ambassadors to Arabia [Egypt, *Marsden*], and caused the caliph's name, in place of his own, to be struck on all the current coin, and prohibited his own name from being included at public worship in the mosques till the caliph's confirmation arrived. In the year 744, a holy person, of the race of the prophet, named Hajy Sayeed Hoormozy [Sirsirri, *Dow* and *Marsden*], returned with the ambassador, and brought a letter from the caliph and a royal dress. The caliph's envoy was met twelve miles outside the city by the king in person, who advanced to receive him on foot, put the letter of the caliph upon his head, and opened it with great solemnity and respect. When he returned into the city, he ordered a grand festival to be made, and caused the public prayers to be said in all the mosques, striking out every king's name from the Khootba who had not been confirmed. Among the number of those degraded monarchs was the king's own father. He even carried his fancy so far as to cause the caliph's name to appear on all his robes and furniture." [14]

The accuracy of the general tenor of this episode in the annals of the reign of Mohammed Tuglak, is sufficiently

[14] This quotation is taken from Brigg's Translation of Ferishtah. It is here adopted in preference to the version given by Marsden, which is undoubtedly more satisfactory, as it appears in its English form, in respect to its explanations of the geographical part of the subject to which it refers, than either the rejected interpretation of Dow or the more trustworthy version of Briggs; but as the object, in these cases, is to reproduce accurately the literal expressions of any author quoted, and not in any way to accept an *amended* MS., or to bend the original text to suit present knowledge, the appended passage is quoted as offering the most exact counterpart of the Persian original now available; the simple point at issue being to select the translator to whose MS. text the greatest confidence is due.

attested by coins Nos. 85, 95, 100, and Nos 86, 110, 111; the former of which bear the simple record of the name of the supposed Egyptian khalif, Al Mostakfi Billah, and the dates, 742, 743, accompanied, in one instance, by a notification of issue from the Delhí mint. The remaining three coins are in like manner superscribed by the sole denomination of Al Abbás Ahmed, the actual recognised khalif of Egypt, and (in two out of the three specimens) are dated 748.

The following is a list of the Egyptian khalifs: —

المستنصر بالله بن الظاهر بالله	inaugurated	659
الحاكم بامر الله ابو العباس احمد	"	660
المستكفي بالله ابو الربيع سليمان	"	701
الواثق بالله ابراهيم	"	740
الحاكم بامر الله ابو العباس احمد بن المستكفي	proclaimed	741
المعتضد بالله ابوبكر	"	753
المتوكل علي الله ابوعبدالله محمد	inaugurated	763
الواثق ابوحفص عمر	"	785
المعتصم بالله ابو يحيي زكريا	"	788
المتوكل *(restored)*	"	791
المستعين بالله ابو الفضل العباس	"	808
المعتضد بالله ابو الفتح داود	"	816
المستكفي بالله ابو الربيع سليمان	"	845
القايم بامرالله ابوالبقا حمزه	"	855
المستنجد بالله ابو المحاسن يوسف	"	859
المتوكل علي الله عبدالعزيز	"	884
المستمسك بالله ابو الصبر يعقوب	"	893
المتوكل علي الله محمد بن يعقوب		doubtful.

The date on coin No. 85, viz. 742, together with that of 741, discovered on a similar coin by Professor Fraehn, indicate that the period fixed by Ferishtah for the development of Mohammed Tuglak's religious doubts should be antedated by two years.

87.—Silver. 141 grs. V.R. Obverse and reverse areas bear the same legends as the gold coin No. 82.

R.—*Marg.* ضرب هذا العدلي بحضرة دهلي سنه خمس و عشرين و سبعمايه This *Udlí* (was) struck at the capital, Delhì, in the year 725.

88.—Silver (much alloyed). 140 grs. C.

Obv.—ضرب في زمن العبد الراجي رحمة الله محمد بن Struck in the time of the servant, trusting in the mercy of God, Mohammed, son of—

R.—السلطان السعيد الشهيد تغلق شاه سنه ثمان و عشرين و سبعمايه The sultan, the fortunate, the testifier, Tughlak Sháh. Year 728.

89—A somewhat similar coin. 136 grs. Dated 730. V.R. The workmanship, however, is much inferior to that of No. 88.

In referring to the early profusion of Mohammed Tuglak, and the enormous sums he is reported to have squandered in gifts and pensions, Ferishtah incidentally alludes to the intrinsic value of the money of this monarch, affirming that —"Nizam ud din Ahmed Bukshy, surprised at the vast sums stated by historians to have been lavished by this prince, took the trouble to ascertain, from authentic records, that these tunkas were of the silver currency of the day, in which was amalgamated a great deal of alloy, so that each tunka only exchanged for sixteen copper pice" (making a tunka worth only about 4*d.* instead of 2*s.*).—*Briggs.*

The main facts of this statement are readily seen to be correct, in the very composition of sundry specimens of the money of Mohammed Tuglak (see coins 88, 89). Though

Ferishtah has been unfortunate in accusing this sultan of making use of debased coin in almost the first transaction of his reign, for even supposing the subsequently adopted system of adulteration to have commenced thus early (which there are stringent reasons for doubting), it could have supplied but a small quota of the enormous amount reported to have been bestowed on this occasion, viz. £2,133,324. Mohammed Tuglak's predecessors too, judging from the invariably pure specimens of their mintages which have survived to contribute their testimony to the point, must be fully exonerated from any charge of debasing the coinage; so that, although Mohammed Tuglak is accused, and justly so, of various frauds upon the circulating medium of his dominions, the reduction of the value of his early largesses by one-fourth is not authorised by the medallic evidence now cited.

90.—Silver. 169 grs. V.R.

Obv.—Sides ابوبكر عمر عثمان علي Abubekr Umur, Usmán, Ulí.

Area—المجاهد في سبيل الله محمد بن تغلق شاه The labourer in the road of God, Mohammed bin Tughlak Sháh.

R.—*Area* لا اله الا الله محمد رسول الله

Marg.—ضرب هذه السكه - - في سنه - عشرين و سبعمايه

91.—Silver, small coin. 56 grs. C.

Obv.—السلطان العادل

R.—٧٢٦ محمد بن تغلق شاه

92.—Silver, small coin. 52 grs.

Obv.—المجاهد في سبيل الله

R.—٧٢ محمد بن تغلقشاه

93.—Silver, small coin. 55 grs. C.

Obv.—الملك و العظمة لله Dominion and greatness are of God.

R.—عبد الراجي محمد تغلق ۷۳۲ (The) servant, the trusting, Mohammed Tughlak. 732.

94.—Silver, small coin. C. 733.

Obv.—الراجي رحمة الله

R.—محمد بن تغلق شنه ثلث و ثلثين و سبعمايه

95.—Silver. 55 grs. V.R.

Obv.— - - خليفةالله في Vicegerent of God in . . .

R.—المستكفي بالله ۷٤۳ Al Mustakfi Billah, 743.

96.—Brass. 136 grs. R. Doulutábad. 730 A.H.

Obv.—مهر شد سكة رائج در روزگار بندۀ اميدوار محمد تغلق
(This piece) was struck (as) a current coin, in the time of the servant, hopeful (of divine mercy), Mohammed Tuglak.

R.—من اطاع السلطان فقد اطاع الرحمن
He who obeys the king, truly he obeys the Merciful (God).

Marg.—در تختگاه دولتاباد سال - ? - هفتصد سي
At the royal residence (capital), Doulutábád, year . . . Seven hundred (and) thirty.

Had Mohammed Tuglak been at all conversant with the modern history of his day, he would probably have hesitated in attempting so radical a change as the introduction of a representative currency, when a similar experiment had but a short time previously (693, H.) been the subject of signal failure in a kingdom not far removed from his own boundaries. Kai Khátou Khan, the Moghul emperor of Persia, had in like manner adopted ideas on the subject from the Chinese, and endeavoured, by the aid of a carefully organised system, and a simultaneous issue of the new notes in the various provinces of his dominions, to enforce the circulation of paper money. The dissatisfaction arising from the measure soon became general, and the inhabitants of the capital (Tabriz) rising as one man, somewhat summarily secured the abrogation of the "Tchao" edict: moreover, the ill-feeling engendered by its temporary experience went far towards the subsequent overthrow of the monarch himself. The following translation of the account of the transaction, which forms the immediate subject of reference, given from the Tubkát Akhberí, is adopted as entering into a more comprehensive detail of the circumstances attendant on this singular episode in the history of Indian finance, than the relation to be found in Ferishtah, which is somewhat unconnected in itself, and appears to confound into one act the separate features of debasing the coinage on the one hand, and the issue of an avowed copper representative of the more precious metals on the other. Ferishtah's narration may be consulted in the translations of Dow and Briggs, vol. i., pp. 282 and 414 respectively.

"The sultan's means did not suffice to satisfy his desires: to gain his ends, therefore, he created a copper currency, ordering coins of that metal to be struck in his mint, after the manner of gold and silver; he then ordained that this copper money should pass current *as* gold and silver, and so should be used in all commercial transactions. The Hindús brought large quantities of copper to the mint and had it coined, and so made for themselves enormous profits; and purchasing goods, and exporting them to other countries, received in exchange gold and silver money. Goldsmiths also manufactured coins in their own houses, and passed them in the bazaars. After some time, things came to such a pass, that, at distant places, the sultan's edict was not observed, and the people took the king's coins only at their intrinsic value in copper, and speculators brought them thence to those parts of the country where the order remained in force, and there exchanged them for gold and silver. In this way the copper currency became by degrees so redundant, that, all at once, it utterly lost credit and was regarded as mere rubbish, while gold and silver became even more precious than before, and commerce was entirely deranged. When the sultan saw that his measure had failed, and that he could not, even by punishment, bring the whole population to obedience, he issued a decree, ordaining that every one who had a royal coin might bring it to the treasury and receive in exchange a gold or silver coin of the old stamp.[15] He thought by this means to restore his copper currency to credit, so that it might be again accepted in exchanges; but the copper money which had been accumulated in people's houses and thrown on one side as worthless, was immediately collected and brought to the treasury to be exchanged for gold and silver coin; and the copper tokens still remained as little current as before, while all the royal treasuries were emptied, and general financial ruin fell upon the whole kingdom."—*Vide Persian MS., Tubkát Akhberi, East India House.*

Many circumstances concur, in demonstrating that the class of coins of which Nos. 96, 97, 98 and 99, are specimens, formed part of the money issued on this peculiar occasion. The causes which lead to this conclusion may be briefly enumerated as follows:—1st. The similarity in weight observable between these coins and the impure silver pieces (Nos. 88, 89) whose place they were seemingly intended to supply: an approximation, it is to be remarked, which does not occur in the previous examples of the silver and copper coinage of this series. 2nd. The shape, which is in a degree assimilated to the assumed prototype; and—3rd. The intrinsic novelty, likewise now for the first time noticeable in the use of brass as a material for coinage. But beyond these minor reasons, there remains the conclusive one of the internal evidence borne by the legends

[15] Mirát al Alem has تنکه زر

on the coins themselves, as seen in the use, in the one case, of the term, "struck as current money," and, in the other, of an inscription fixing the relative value of the piece impressed: intimations unsanctioned by custom, and, which it is needless to say, a full intrinsic metallic value would have rendered superfluous.

It is probable that many other coins, composed of a similar admixture of metals, and bearing legends in a measure appropriate to the occasion, constituted a portion of the forced currency of Mohammed Tuglak; it may be advisable to advert concisely to each in detail. As regards No. 100, the identity of date and metal, accompanied by the retention of a portion of the same legend as No. 96, sufficiently indicates that a similar object attended the mintage of both. In the case of No. 101, the two first of these points of similarity equally exist, and the inscriptions in themselves counsel due obedience to the sovereign, who, in the issue of the money, thus heavily tried the subservience of his subjects. The signs of agreement with the adopted sample of this representative coinage, to be detected in Nos. 102 and 103 are less prominent, and are confined to a coincidence in date and metal: however, on the supposition that in a comprehensive scheme, such as the present is shown to have been, it would have been necessary to provide proportionate substitutes for the smaller silver pieces; the specimens now cited may fairly claim admittance into the series under review. Nos. 104 and 105, under different forms of inscription to those employed on other coins of the class, bear full signs of their definite purpose, and in their respective record of جائز "current," "lawful," and شرعي "legal," amply manifest the design with which they were produced.

The dates on these coins are sufficiently in unison with

the information to be gathered from *written* history, not to militate in any way against the validity of the opinion now advanced, as to the occasion to which the money in question owes its origin. The evidence of Indian authors, however, as to the exact time at which the first issue of brass tokens took place, or as to the period during which this Substitute system remained in force, is greatly deficient; and the several narratives of the Tubkát Akhberí, the Mirát al Alem, and the chronicles of Ferishtah, all fail in this respect: from the coins themselves, therefore, must be sought an elucidation of these doubtful points.

It will be seen that the brass coins already classed under the head of Mohammed Tuglak's forced currency, uniformly bear one of three dates, either 730, 731, or 732: the first of these is to be found on full six-tenths of the whole of the very numerous specimens available for reference; next in order of abundance is to be seen the annual date of 731; and, lastly, the number 732 is but rarely met with: implying, if such testimony is trustworthy, a very extensive fabrication during the first, and, apparently commencing year, sufficiently supported during the second, and followed by a remarkable diminution in the issue of the third year. It may be assumed, therefore, that 730 A.H., witnessed the first vigorous effort at the introduction of the new currency, well sustained during 731, and failing entirely in 732. The limitation here assigned to the survival of this Indian adaptation of the Chinese Tchao system, is curiously supported both in the negative as well as direct evidence, deducible from the *real* money of Mohammed Tuglak. The ample materials at command, admit of the abundant and unbroken numismatic illustration of each of the first thirteen years of the reign of this prince, of the *dated* coins thus capable of being cited, scarcely a solitary instance of either *gold or silver* money occurs bearing the dates 730 or 731.[16] It has been already shown that the brass money was manufactured *only* during 730, 731, and part of 732; and, to complete the chain and fill up the years both initiative and conclusive of this financial change, the silver coins, Nos. 89 and 93, may be quoted as bearing respectively the annual dates of 730 and 732. Hence, as far as may be judged from present proofs, it would appear that, during the continuance of the decree giving effect to the forced currency, but few, if any, gold or silver coins were fabricated at either the Delhí or Doulatábád mints; and that as its introduction had been attended by a discontinuance of the use of precious metals, so the withdrawal of the ordinance is simultaneously marked, by a reappearance of a due proportionate amount the usual circulating medium.

97.—Brass. 139 grs. V.C. Delhí, 731 A.H.

Obv.—Similar legend to No. 96.

℞.—*Area*, legend as above, No. 96.

Marg.—در تختگاد دهلي سال - - هفتصد سي يک

98.—Brass. R. Delhí, 732 A.H.[17]

Similar to No. 97, with هفتصد سي دو

---

[16] There is one silver coin, and one only, in the present collection, similar in type to No. 94, but of very debased metal; the date on which may possibly be read 731. The inscription is imperfectly executed, and the word احد if such it be, is so peculiarly formed that it can scarcely be relied on as representing that number.

[17] Many specimens of the coins described under Nos. 96, 97, 98, bear very distinct signs of being the production of dies other than those in use at the royal mints, and are probably some of the forgeries alluded to in the extract from the Tubkát Akhberí.

99.—Brass. 138 grs. V.R. Doulutábád, 732 A.H. B.M.[18]

Obv.—مهر شد سکه پنجاه کاني در روزگار بنده اميدوار محمد تغلق Struck as a piece of fifty káńís,[19] in the time of the servant, hopeful (of divine mercy), Mohammed Tughlak.

R.—*Area*, as No. 96.

Marg.—و - - درتخت گاه دولت اباد سال

100.—Brass. 112 grs. V.C.

Obv.—٧٣٠ محمد من اطاع السلطان

He who obeys the king, Mohammed, 730—

R.—تغلق فقد اطاع الرحمن

Truly he obeys the Merciful, Tughlak.

101.—Brass. 112 grs. C. Date 730.

Obv.—٧٣٠ محمد اطيعوا الله و اطيعوا الرسول واولي الامر منكم

Obey God, and obey the Prophet, and those (who are) in authority among you (4th chap. Korán), Mohammed, 730.

R.— لايولا السلطان كل الناس بعضهم بعضاً تغلق

Sovereignty is not conferred upon every man, (but) some (are placed over) others, Tughlak.

102.—Brass. 66 grs. C.

Obv.—محمد بن تغلق

R.—٧٣٠ ضرب الربعي

103.—Brass. 55 grs. C.

Obv.—عبد محمد بن تغلق

R.—٧٣٠ حسبي ربي

---

[18] The value of the pretended exactitude of Ferishtah's dates is somewhat shaken by the coins Nos. 96 and 99. The former of which proves most obviously that Deogír had become the *royal city of Doulutábád* in the year 730, whereas Ferishtah expressly assigns this intitulation to the year 739. See Briggs and Dow, A.H. 739.

[19] Káni, probably the "jetul" of Ferishtah, see ante, page 36.

104.—Brass. 74 grs. U.

Obv.—(بنده امیدوار ?) سکّه زر جائز در عهد[20]

R.—*Centre* محمّد تغلق

Marg.—श्री: मोहमद[21]

105.—Brass. 84 grs. V.R.

Obv.—ضرب الدرهم الشرعي في زمن العبد محمد بن تغلق[22]

Struck (as) a legal dirhem, in the time of the servant Mohammed bin Tughlak.

R.—بدار الاسلام في سنه ثلثين و سبعمايه

At the seat of Islámism, in the year 730.

106.—Brass. 82 grs. R.

Obv. as No. 106.

R.—بحضره دهلي في سنه ثلثين و سبعمايه At the capital, Delhí, in the year 730.

107.—Copper. 53 grs. V.R.

Obv.—المُلْكُ و العِزّة لله Dominion and glory are of God.

R.—*Centre* محمّد تغلق

Marg.—سال - - هفتصد سي دو 732.

---

[20] The second letter of زر has been restored. The word زر assuming it to be such, seems to have been used in this instance in its generic sense of money, rather than in its distinguishing meaning of gold: the brass representatives of the gold dinárs have yet to be brought to light.

[21] The *o* in *Mohamad* is expressed in what is now known as the *Bengali* form of that vowel.

[22] The ش in الشرعي is assumed from other and clearer specimens of the coin than that which appears in the plate, which has been selected for the engraver, from its affording a more general outline of the whole legend than other pieces of the same class.

108.—Copper. 68 grs.

Obv.—السّلطان ظل الله The sultan, shadow of God.

℞.—محمّد بن تغلقشاه Mohammed bin Tuglak Sháh.

109.—Silver and copper mixed. 132 grs. U.

Obv.—الامام الاعظم خليفه اللّه

℞.—*Centre* المستكفي بالله اميرالمومنين

Marg. illegible.

110.—Copper. 128 grs. R. 748 A.H.

Obv.—الحاكم بامرالله سنه ٧٤٨

℞.—ابو العباس احمد

111.—Brass. 55 grs. V.R.

Legend and date similar to No. 109.

Twentieth King (A.H. 752—790; A.D. 1351—1388).

On the 27th of Muhurrum, 752, Hindústán was relieved from the capricious rule of Mohammed bin Tuglak, and the vacant throne was filled by his cousin, Fírúz. In 754, the new monarch attempted to reduce Haji Ilias, who had thrown off his allegiance to the house of Delhí, and assumed regal honors as sovereign of Bengal and Behar: the emperor was, however, able to accomplish little or nothing towards the subjection of his revolted subject; and, not long afterwards, the kingdom of Bengal became effectively independent. In 755, Fírúz commenced the first of those magnificent public works which have perpetuated his name, while those of far mightier kings have been forgotten: the remains of many of these undertakings are still to be seen, scattered, in no scant proportion, over the face of northern Hindústán: indeed, in the original bed of a canal, first excavated by this monarch, at this day flow the waters of the Jumna, which irrigate the surrounding country, from the foot of the Sewalik, to Hissar; and a more modern branch from which supplies the present denizens of the once imperial city of Delhí.

Fruitful in solid benefits to his subjects and succeeding generations, the long and prosperous reign of Fírúz has afforded but slight materials for the historian: hence Ferishtah's narrative of his rule is almost confined to the enumeration of the roads, wells, canals, etc., which, to this time, in bearing the name of Fírúz, have, as yet, scarce needed a chronicler.

In the year 789, the sultan, suffering from the increasing infirmities incident to his advanced age, associated his son, Násir ud din, in the government of the empire; and, from this time, the public prayers were recited in the joint names of father and son. The arrangement thus completed was but of brief duration: a revolt in the capital resulted in the flight of the prince and the reassumption of regal power by the father; who, however, again as quickly resigned it to a grandson, Ghiás ud din, son of Futteh Khán, who finally succeeded to the empire on the decease of Fírúz, which event took place in 790.

112.—Gold. 167 grs. R. (B. M.)

Obv.—واثق بتائيد يزداني فيروز شاه سلطاني

Confiding in the benignity of God, the royal Fírúz Sháh.

R.—ضربت هذه السكة في زمان الامام ابو العباس احمد

خلدت ملكه This coin was struck in the time of the Imám Abúl Abbás Ahmed. May his sovereignty endure

113.—Gold. 170 grs. (B. M.)

Obv.—السّطان الاعظم سيف امير المومنين ابوالمظفر فيروز شاه السّلطان خلدت ملكه The most mighty sultan, sword of the commander of the faithful, Abul Muzafar Fírúz Sháh, the sultan. May his reign be prolonged.

R.—في زمان الامام امير المومنين ابو الفتح خلدت خلافته In the time of the Imám, commander of the faithful, Abúl Fateh. May his khalifat endure.

Marg.—ضربت هذه السكّة بحضر - - ين و سبعمايه

The assumption by Fírúz, at this particular juncture, of the title of Seif Amír Al Mominín, as connected with the simultaneous recognition of the new Egyptian khalif, Abul Fateh Abubekir, who had only lately attained pontifical honors, seems to indicate that the title in question was the one conferred upon the former on the occasion of his investiture with the dress of honor, which was received at the court of Delhí in 757.

114.—Gold. 167 grs. Small coin. Date 788.

Obv.—سّلطاني فيروز شاه

R.—نايب امير المومنين ٧٨٨

115.—Silver and copper mixed. 141 grs. Date 773.

Obv.—فيروز شاه سّلطاني ضربت بحضرت دهلي

R.—الخليفه امير المومنين خلد خلافته ٧٧٣

116.—Copper and silver. 136 grs. Date 791.

Obv.—فيروز شاه ظفر سّلطاني ضربت بحضرت دهلي

R.—الخليفه ابوعبد الله خلدت خلافته ٧٩١

117.—Silver and copper. 54 grs.

Obv.—فيروز شاه سّلطاني خلد ملّكه

R.—الخليفه ابو الفتح خلدت خلافته

118.—Silver and copper. 140 grs. Date 784.
Obv. as No. 114.

R.—الخليفه ابو عبد الله خلدت خلافته ٧٨٤

119.—Copper. 68 grs.
Obv. as No. 118.

R.—دار الملك دهلي

120.—Copper. 36 grs.

Obv.—فيروز سلطاني

R.—بحضرت دهلي

121.—Copper. 55 grs.

Obv.—فيروز شاه سلطاني

R.—ابو العباس احمد

122 and 123.—Coins similar in types and legends to No. 115, bear respectively the dates ٨١٦ 816, and ٨١٧ 817.

The appearance of two coins, dated severally *twenty-six and twenty-seven* years subsequent to the decease of the monarch whose name they bear, is not a little remarkable. Adverting to the previous history of Moslem Asiatic nations, the simple fact of the fabrication of money, displaying the titles of any given sovereign, continuing for a brief period immediately following his death, occasions no surprise: hence No. 116 is readily accepted as a posthumous coin of this class; but the lapse of more than a quarter of a century observable in the instances of Nos. 122 and 123, in placing these pieces so much beyond the limit usually admissible in parallel cases, leads to an enquiry whether unusual causes may not have led to their production. It is known that the issue of this species of coinage, though probably not *completely* serial, was renewed at divers times between the fixed periods of 790 and 816, as evidenced by specimens extant in the possession of Captain Cunningham, bearing dates 801 and 804.

The facts available, together with the unassailable evidence of the coins themselves, seem to necessitate a conclusion that, during the whole, or a portion of each of the years 801, 804, 816, and 817, if not during many of the intermediate ones, the dominant possessor of the city of Delhí issued money in the name of a previous king; ensuring, by this means, at the very least, a ready and unquestioned circulation of the coinage thus put forth, the counterpart of which must, at the time, have formed the bulk of the circulating medium of the Delhí empire. As, however, this inference involves the deduction that either these parties coined no money in their own names, or, striking money of their own, were careless of this usually highly-prized right, it becomes necessary to examine whether it is possible that the individuals who, at each of these several marked periods held sway in the metropolis of Hindústán, should have submitted to the use of the titles of other kings on money issuing from the mint over which they maintained control. As regards the epochs of 801 and 804, it is to be remarked, that after the departure of Tímúr, and the subsequent speedy expulsion of Nusserut Sháh, the city of Delhí passed into the hands of Mullú Yekbal Khán, who retained possession of the town till his death, in 807. Though this chief acted entirely on his own account, and, as will be shown hereafter, considerably augmented his territories, it is nowhere asserted that he either coined money in his own name, or assumed any of the usual insignia of royalty. A difficulty might suggest itself in this place, in the fact of the continued existence of Mahmúd, a monarch duly inaugurated on the throne of Hindústán, who had fled to Guzrát on the capture of the metropolis by the

Moghuls. Yekbal Khán does not, however, appear at any period after the departure of the Moghul host, to have, either directly or indirectly, acknowledged Mahmúd as sultan; indeed, it is by no means unlikely, that during the early part of his own independent rule, he should actually have discouraged any such recognition. It may, therefore, be assumed as highly probable, that to supply the currency requisite for the ordinary monetary transactions of his people, Yekbal Khán, having no pretence to strike coin in his own name, and no predilection to perpetuate the name of a king he was in effect supplanting, may have adopted the expedient of issuing pieces similar to those of Fírúz, and still emblazoned with his titles; the like of which, to judge by the present comparative abundance of the specimens extant, must have formed a very considerable proportion of the total currency of the day. Referring to the period comprised in the two years 816 and 817, it is singular that during the first fifteen months of this time, it is also, at the least, doubtful whether any *king* reigned in Delhi. Mahmúd dying in 815, left no successor to the throne: the chief power in the state shortly afterwards fell to the lot of Daulat Khán Lodí: his actual assumption of regal honors, however, despite the directly expressed assertion of Ferishtah to that effect, is at the best highly problematical. This point, also, will be more fully noticed in its proper place; in the meantime, it may be adverted to as possibly bearing directly upon the present enquiry, in respect to the hitherto inexplicable non-discovery of any money displaying the name of the ruler in qnestion. Daulat Khán surrendered to Khizr Khán in the third month of 817 A. H. Here, again, it is perhaps doing no violence to probabilities, remarking both the absence of any extant coin of Daulat Khán conjoined with the doubt of his kingship, and the clear testimony of the dates on coins Nos. 122, 123, to suppose that this chief, in imitation of the practice of a predecessor, issued coin in the name of Firúz.

COINS BEARING THE JOINT NAMES OF FIRUZ AND HIS SON ZIFFER.

124.—Copper and silver. 78 grs.

Obv.—فيروز شاه ظفر ابن فيروز شاه

℞.—ابو عبد الله خلدت خلافته

125.—Silver and copper. 78 grs. Coin bearing similar legends to the above, but the produce of different dies.

The above coins are, it will be seen, struck in the joint names of Fírúz and his son Ziffer: as it is known that Fírúz, in 760 A.H., conferred "the ensigns of royalty on his son, Futteh Khán," and that Mohammed, the second son, was, in 789 A.H., raised to the throne during the life-time of his father, it is by no means improbable that, in the like spirit, the third son should have been allowed to adopt so much of kingly rank as was implied in the exhibition of his name on the coinage, in the government over which he presided. There is much obscurity prevailing in Ferishtah, consequent upon an apparent confusion of two different persons bearing the title of Ziffer Khán. It is not perhaps requisite to enter into a detailed enquiry on the subject, as, notwithstanding the uncertainty which of necessity remains, there seems to be but little question, that the prince now sought to be identified, was *the Ziffer Khán*, governor of Mahobah (Bundelkund), who was so hastily despatched by the vizir on the occasion of the attack upon the latter's house by the Prince Mohammed, in 789 A.H.

Twenty-First King (A.H. 790—791; A.D. 1388—1389).

The rule of Ghiás ud din Tuglak II. demands but brief notice, its events being told in the record, on the one hand, of the lax indulgence of the monarch, and, on the other, of his unavailing pursuit of the late joint-king Násir ud din. The sultan, having alarmed the nobles of his own court, a conspiracy was formed which put a period to his life and sway, little more than five months after his first attainment of the latter.

126.—Silver and copper. 136 grs. A.H. 790.

Obv.—تغلق شاه سلطاني ضربت بحضرت دهلي

R.—الخليفه ابو عبد الله خلدت خلافته ۷۹۰

127.—Silver and copper. 80 grs.

Obv.—تغلق شاه سلطاني خلد ملك

R.—ابو عبد الله خلدت خلافته

128.—Copper. 68 grs.

Obv.—تغلق شاه سلطاني

R.—دار الملك دهلي

Twenty-Second King (A.H. 791—793; A.D. 1389—1390).

Abúbekir, the son of Ziffer, and grandson of Fírúz, was raised to the throne on the death of Tuglak II. The history of this reign is also comprised in but few words, being marked almost solely by the successful counteraction by the king, of the treasonable designs of his vizir, followed by the advance of Násir ud din; who, after various intermediate turns of fortune, once again sat on the throne of his father.

129.—Silver and copper. 134 grs. A.H. 791.

Obv.— ابوبکر شاه بن ظفر بن فیروز شاه سلطاني

℞.— الخليفه ابوعبد الله خلدت خلافته ۷۹۱

Coins of this type are extant bearing the several dates of 791, as above, and 792, and 793, A.H.

130.—Copper. 114 grs.

Obv.—In a square area ابو بکر شاه

Marg.— ظفر بن فیروز شاه سلطاني

℞.— نایب امیر المومنین ۷۹۲

131.—Copper. 155 grs. Imperfect

Obv.—In a circular area ابو بکر شاه

Marg.— فیروز شاه - - -

℞. as No. 130.

132.—Silver and copper. 47 grs. Small coin, obverse and reverse legends similar to No. 129.

133.—Copper. 58 grs.

Obv.— ابو بکر شاه ظفر سلطاني

℞.— الخليفه ابو عبد الله خلدت خلافته

Twenty-third King (A.H. 793—796; A.D. 1390—1394).

The supremacy of Násir ud din Mohammed as sole monarch of Hindústán, which dates properly from Ramzán, 793, to Rubbi us Sani, 796, does not offer much matter for remark.

In the early part of the reign, the governor of Guzrát rebelled, but was subdued by the sultan's generals; as also were the Rahtor Rájpúts, who shortly afterwards attempted to throw off their allegiance. Doubts having been suggested as to the faith of his vizir, the emperor hastened to meet the difficulty, and, by prompt action, secured himself against the possible consequences. A fever, aggravated by the exertions it was necessary to make to suppress an insurrection in Mewát, brought the career of this monarch to a close.

134.—Silver. 173 grs. (*Marsden's Cabinet, B.M.*)

Obv.—السّلطان الاعظم ابوالمحامد محمّد شاه فيروزشاه سلّطاني

The most mighty sovereign, Abúl Muhámed, Mohammed Sháh, (son of) the royal Fírúz Sháh.

℞.— في زمن الامام امير المومنين خلدت خلافته

In the time of the Imám, commander of the faithful. May his khalifat endure.

135.—Impure silver. 167 grs. Date 795.

Obv.—محمّد شاه فيروز شاه سلّطاني

℞.—*Centre* ابو عبد الله

Marg.— ۷۹۵ خلدت خلافته ضربت بحضرت دهلي

136.—Silver and copper. 140 grs. Date 793. (Others are dated 794 and 795.)

Obv.—محمّد شاه فيروز شاه سلّطان

℞.—۷۹۳ الخليفه ابو عبد الله خلدت خلافته

137.—Copper. 140 grs. Date 793 H.

Obv.—*Centre* محمّد شاه

Marg.—ضربت بحضرت دهلي

℞.—۷۹۳ نايب امير المومنين

138.—Copper. 68 grs. Small coin. 793.

Obv.—محمّد شاه سلّطاني

℞.—۷۹۳ دار الملك دهلي

139.—Copper. 52 grs.

Obv.—محمد شاه فيروز شاه سلطان

℞.— - الخليفه ابو عبد الله

TWENTY-FOURTH KING (A.H. 796; A.D. 1394).

Humáyún, the son of Násir ud din, assumed, on his accession, the designation of Sekunder Shah. The historical record of the rule of this sovereign is confined to the announcement, that he attained regal honors and enjoyed them for the brief space of forty-five days.

140.—Silver and copper mixed. 142 grs. Date 795.[23]

Obv.—سكندر شاه محمد شاه سلطاني

℞.—٧٩٥ الخليفه ابو عبد الله خلدت خلافته

141.—Copper. 134 grs. Date 795.

Obv.—*Centre* سكندر شاه

Marg. - - بحضرت

℞.—٧٩٥ نايب امير المومنين

---

[23] The unit numeral on coin No. 140, displays a singular form of the figure ٥ *five :* it is somewhat strange to find this novel style of the figure in use almost simultaneously with the old five, to be observed on coin No. 135, which has, up to this time, been in no way distinguishable from a naught, as disclosed on No. 126. It is certainly possible that, in this particular instance, the employment of the unit numeral on the second coin may refer to the naught of 790, during part of which year Nasir ud din Mohammed was the effective sultan, in nominal conjunction with his father Firúz; but there are many reasons for doubting the probability that the coin in question should have been produced under the joint auspices of Firúz and Mohammed. Be this as it may, there can be no difficulty in admitting the fact, that the figure more immediately under notice represents a five, as both its present and its subsequent use clearly demonstrate that it can be no other numeral.

It is here necessary to rectify an error which has occurred in the assignment of the value of a numeral similar to that now

142.—Copper. 67 grs.

Obv.— سكندر شاه سلطاني

R.—٧٩٥ دار الملك دهلي

---

referred to, which is to be seen occupying the place of the terminal figure of the annual date on the coin of Umur, No. 63. On a hasty examination, and adverting more particularly to the hitherto unquestioned date of the accession of this prince (716 A.H.), the late period in the year at which this event was placed, as well as to the brief duration of the reign itself, which barely extended into a second year, the value of this strange figure was accepted with little hesitation from the requirements of written history. Added to this, the absence of any apparent similitude with any of the other nine recognised numerals, and the facile transition from the correctly formed Persian ٦ to a character having a final flourish instead of an accurately prolonged perpendicular termination, seemed to explain the process whence the numeral derived its origin. The present collation of a more extensive series of specimens, bearing this character in a but slightly altered form, led to a doubt as to the due identification of its functions in the previous instance; and the result of this investigation has proved most decisively that whatever may have been the derivation, or the original design which attended the use of the figure, its subsequent employment could only refer to the number *five*. Marsden (p. 550) had already shown that a somewhat similar symbol was used to represent this number towards the close of the supremacy of the Afghán dynasty in India; and now, tracing this numeral in its little varied shape, upwards through the well-developed instances afforded by the coins of Behlól, Sekunder, and others, there remains no possible obstacle to the recognition of its use in a similar signification on the coin of Umur. On the other hand, in the progress of the enquiry resulting from the attempt to verify the history of the Patán domination in Hindústán, too much reason has been found to distrust Ferishtah's accuracy, to make it necessary to pause in discrediting his *given date* in the present instance. In conclusion, it may be appropriate to endeavour to trace the derivation of this anomalous form of the Persian ٥. Admitting a difficulty previously noticed, regarding the want of sufficient distinction between the Persian ٠ *naught* and the ٥ *five* once in use at Delhi, it is not improbable that the necessity of a more obvious means of discriminating the expression of these two numbers may have led to the adoption of the more purely local Devanagri ५ *five*, as a substitute for the Indo-Persian form of that figure. The Nágrí *five* approximates closely, especially in its cursive shape, to

TWENTY-FIFTH KING (A.H. 796—815; A.D. 1394—1413).

On the death of Sekunder Sháh, the nobles of the court elevated to the musnud his brother, Mahmúd, a minor. The very commencement of this nominal supremacy was marked by misfortunes; and the real weakness of the empire was increased by insurrections which sprang up on all sides: among the rest is to be noticed the important defection of the vizir, Khwaja Jehán, who, in this act, founded the temporarily powerful kingdom of Jánpúr. In 797 A.H., a new claimant to the throne was advanced, in the person of Nuserut Khán, a son of Futteh Khán, and grandson of Fírúz; and his supporters actually took and retained possession of the new portion of the capital denominated Fírúzábád, while Mahmúd and his followers held the old town of Delhí. In this anomalous state matters continued for the space of three years, each being in a measure king, and each holding his own dependent provinces of the empire: meanwhile, constant and sanguinary encounters occurred between the troops of the rival factions. At length, Mullú Yekbál Khan, who, in fit keeping with the whole of this strange proceeding, had remained an observant and neutral spectator, first deceived, and, for the time, ruined Nuserut Sháh, and then succeeded in getting possession of the person of Mahmúd, in whose name he thenceforth pretended to rule. This uncertain government was how-

---

the early style of the adaptation of the numeral displayed on coin No. 63; but the *five* on the coins of Shír and Islám is so far changed that, read as a Nágrí figure, it would stand for a very correct *six*. A figure but slightly differing from the form employed on the coins of Shír is known to have supplied the place of a *four* on the Turkish money of the twelfth century A.H., and many of our modern founts of Persian type possess no other representative of this number. An instance of its use may be seen in the printed description of coin No. 95.

ever put an end to by the advance of the celebrated Tímúr: the defeat of the Indian army, the surrender and subsequent merciless sack of Delhí followed; and, for five days, the Moghul conqueror continued feasting while his troops destroyed; and, to finish the inconsistency, "on the day of his departure he offered up to the Divine Majesty his sincere and humble tribute of grateful praise." The capital of Hindústán remained in a state of complete anarchy, to which were superadded the horrors of famine and pestilence, for the space of two months after the departure of Tímúr: at the end of this period, it was taken possession of by Nuserut Sháh, and, shortly afterwards, it again passed into the hands of Mullú Yekbál Khán, whose sway at this time, extended but little beyond its walls: the provinces being, in effect, independent under their several governors, who, one and all, styled themselves kings. Yekbál Khán, nevertheless, succeeded in gradually enlarging his boundaries; and, in 804, was joined by Mahmúd (who had fled at the sack of Delhí to Guzrát), on whom he bestowed his protection and *a pension*. Yekbál Khán now undertook an expedition against Ibrahím Sháh Sherkí, the sultán of Jánpúr; and Mahmúd, thinking to improve his own condition, went over to Ibrahim: he was, however, received with but small encouragement, and, finally, was allowed by both parties to establish himself as a sort of local king of Kanój. On the death of Yekbál Khán, which took place in an action with Khizr Khán, the governor of Multán, Mahmúd was again invited to Delhí; but "deficient both in sense and courage," he made but little profit of his new position, and at last died in Zulkád, 815.[24]

---

[24] The date of the death of Mahmúd is fixed by Ferishtah at the 11th Zulkád, 814 A.H.; and the assumption of power by Daulat Khán Lodí, is affirmed, by the same author, to have taken place

143.—Silver. 174 grs.

Obv.—السلطان الاعظم ابو المحامد محمود شاه محمد شاه فيروز شاه سلطاني The most mighty sovereign Abúl Muhámed Mahmúd Sháh, (son of) Mohammed Sháh, (son of) the royal Fírúz Sháh.

℞.— —— في زمن الامام امير المومنين خلدت خلافته ——
In the time of the Imám, commander of the faithful. May his khalifat endure.

144.—Silver (impure). 141 grs. Date 796.

Obv.—محمود شاه محمد شاه سلطاني

℞.—٧٩٦ الخليفه ابو عبد الله خلدت خلافته

145.—Copper. 140 grs. Date 813.

Obv.—*Centre* محمود شاه

Marg. illegible.

℞.—٨١٣ نايب امير المومنين

---

on the 1st of Muhurrum, 816. A difficulty is suggested in the very fact of the capital, and the country dependent upon it, having, as thus shown, remained for fourteen months without even a nominal ruler: this anomaly, moreover, is not attempted to be met by the writer in question, nor is even its existence noticed. (See Briggs, vol. i. page 504; Elphinstone, vol. ii. page 80).

The Tubkat Akberí gives the following explanation of the circumstances and dates bearing upon the matter, which, in satisfactorily accounting for what Ferishtah has left unexplained, seems, in so doing, to point out his error, as having arisen from a substitution of the year 814 for 815, as the period of the decease of Mahmúd:—

"After the death of Mahmúd, in Zulkad, 815, for two months anarchy prevailed in Delhí, when the nobles of that prince entered into a compact with Daulat Khan, and Mulik Ardríz and Mubáriz Khán passed over from Khizr Khán and joined Daulat Khán," etc.

The Mirát ul Alem also gives 815 as the year of Mahmúd's death; though it openly mentions some uncertainty as existing in regard to the extent of his reign, which is noted at "twenty *or* twenty-two years and two months."

146.—Copper. 56 grs.

Obv.—Legend as No. 144.

R.—الخليفه امير المومنين خلدت خلافته

147.—Copper. 68 grs. Date 815 A.H. (See note [24].)

Obv.—محمود شاه سلطاني

R.—دار الملك دهلي ۸۱۵

TWENTY-SIXTH KING (A.H. 797; A.D. 1395).

The history of the partial sovereignty of Nuserut Sháh, including both his three years' possession of Fírúzabad, and his momentary occupation of the metropolis after the departure of Tímúr, has been sufficiently adverted to in the notice of the reign of Mahmúd.

From 802, Nuserut Sháh appears to have been lost sight of by Indian historians, though his coin, No. 151, would seem to indicate at least a temporary renewal of his power in 807 H.

148.—Copper. 143 grs.

Obv.—نصرت شاه سلطاني

R.—نايب امير المومنين

149.—Copper. 57 grs.

Obv.—نصرت شاه سلطاني

R.—دار الملك دهلي

150.—Copper. 67 grs. Date 797.

Obv. as above.

R.—دار الملك دهلي ۷۹۷

151.—Copper. 67 grs. Date 807. Similar to No. 150.

Other coins bear date 798.

Twenty-seventh King (A.H. 815—817; 1413—1414).

Whatever may have been the nominal designation under which Daulat Khán Lodí held the government of Delhí, the actual power pertaining to his office, whether monarchical or oligarchical, seems to have been but limited. Of the fifteen months allotted by historiaus as the duration of his chieftainship, eleven were occupied in petty attempts to extend his confined boundaries, and the remaining four were passed in suffering a siege, in the citadel of Delhí, and vainly opposing the arms of Khizr Khán, who, at the end of this time succeeded in putting an end to the somewhat doubtful sovereignty of his adversary.

The absence of any specimens of the coinage of Daulat Khán Lodí can hardly be said to cause surprise: on the one hand, his circumscribed rule and embarrassed circumstances must have gone far to limit any fabrication of his individual coins, and, on the other, the plunder of the metropolis and the surrounding country by the hordes of Timúr must, as it depopulated, have utterly for the time impoverished the narrow dominion over which alone Daulat Khán held sway. This country, moreover, was peculiarly *the* portion of all Hindústán the most afflicted by the inroad of the Moghuls. Added to this, were it not for the direct assertion of Ferishtah, that Daulat Khán assumed royal insignia, and struck coin in his own name, the tenor of the narrations of other authors might suggest some doubt on the subject:[25] a doubt that is naturally increased by the discovery of two coins impressed with the name of another monarch,

---

[25] Abúl Fazl does not allow Daulat Lodí a place in the list of the monarchs of Hindústán, though he mentions that the government was held by this chief for a limited period.

struck in the capital of which Daulat Khán was nominal lord, and dated one in each of the years during nearly the whole of the first, and a portion of the second, of which his sway endured.

Twenty-eighth King (a.h. 817—824; a.d. 1414—1421).

Khizr Khán's accession to the dignity of ruler of the imperial city and the small tract now subject to it, in adding thereto his own governmental provinces of the Punjáb, had the effect of again increasing the importance of the empire of the metropolis. Khizr having accepted service under Timúr, and having held his government of Multan, etc., from that conqueror, continued to acknowledge the supremacy of the dynasty of the Moghul after he had himself obtained possession of the capital. The new viceroy was enabled to assert a sway much more extended than could have been expected from the unsatisfactory state to which the monarchy of Delhí had been reduced consequent upon the inroad of Timúr; and his power, though unequal, was sufficiently recognised according to Indian notions of government. At his death, he was in a condition to secure the peaceful transmission of his honors to his son, Mubárik, who, apparently with the sanction of the nobles of the court, again revived the kingly style.

The following extracts show that Khizr Khán, in declining to assume the title of sultan, refrained from exercising that first of Oriental privileges of sovereignty, involved in the inscription of his own name on the money of the country.

It would certainly have been satisfactory, in referring to the subjoined assertions of the acknowledgment of Timúr and his successor, to have been able to have cited direct numismatic proof of the Moghul supremacy in Hindústán: however, it is probable that Khizr Khán did not needlessly multiply such records of his own subservience.

"He refrained from assuming royal titles, and gave out that he held the government for Timúr, in whose name he caused the coin to be struck and the Khutba to be read. After the death of Timúr, the Khutba was read in the name of his successor, Sháh Rokh Mírza; to whom he sometimes even sent tribute at his capital of Samarkand."—*Briggs' Ferishtah*, vol. i. page 508.

"Khizr Khán, out of gratitude to his benefactor, Timúr, did not assume the title of sultan, but continued to have the Khotbah read in the name of that monarch, contenting himself with being styled Ayáut Aála, or The Most High in Dignity. At the death of Timúr, the Khotbah was read in the name of his successor, Sháh Rokh, concluding with a prayer for the prosperity of Khizr Khán." —*Gladwin's Ayin i Akberi.*

TWENTY-NINTH KING (A.H. 824—839; A.D. 1421—1435).

The annals of the period during which the now re-established throne of Delhi was filled by Muaz ud din Mubárik, are distinguished by a little varying succession of efforts on the part of the sovereign to repress the continual revolts of his subjects: prominent among these is to be noticed the pertinacious and daring opposition of Jusserut Gukka, who, during the thirteen years of Mubárik's reign, appeared in arms and fought well contested campaigns no less than six several times. The rebellion of Fouládis also noticeable, not so much on account of its own intrinsic importance as from the disastrous results which attended the introduction of the Moghul auxiliaries of Ali, the governor of Kábul on the part of Sháh Rokh, whose aid was invoked by Foulád as a means of extricating himself from his own difficulties. Mubárik was assassinated in 839, by a band of Hindús employed for that purpose by his own vizir.

152.—[25]

153.—Copper. 172 grs.

Obv.—Area مبارك شاه

Marg.—سلطان ضربت بحضرت دهلي

R.—٨٣- نايب امير المومنين

154.—Copper. 80 grs.

Obv.—سلطان مبارك شاه

R.—٨٣٢ دارالملك دهلي

155.—Copper. 40 grs.

Obv.—مبارك شاه

R.— - - بحضرت

---

[25] The electrotype cast of the coin figured as No. 152, was placed in the hands of the engraver before an opportunity was afforded of submitting it to any critical examination, under the impression that the original was an unquestionable coin of Muaz ud din Mubárik. On a closer scrutiny, the name of the mint city (the capital of eastern Bengal), and the surviving word of the date (*50), are found to render this assignment somewhat dubious; over and above this difficulty, the question as to whom the coin really does belong, is not readily soluble by the evidence of written history, inasmuch as the kingdom of Bengal is stated to have been held by Hájí Iliás from 744 to 760 (Stewart, pp. 83, 86; Briggs, vol. iv. p. 331); and from 830 to 862, by Nasir Sháh (Stewart, p. 100); or, according to Ferishtah, by Yusuf, from 849 to 866 (Briggs, vol. iv. p. 339). Under these circumstances, the bare description of the coin is appended without further comment.

Silver. 162 grs. U. (*Dr. Swiney*).

Obv.—السلطان الاعظم معز (?فخر) الدنيا و الدين ابو المظفر مبارکشاه السلطان

R.—*Area* يمين الخليفه ناصر امير المومنين

Marg.—سكه بحضرة جلال سنارکانو سنه خمسين و

At the royal capital, Sunargaon, year * 50.

THIRTIETH KING (A.H. 839—849; A.D. 1435—1444).

On the death of Mubárik, the vizir, assassin of that monarch, elevated as his puppet king, Mohammed bin Feríd, a grandson of Khizr Khán. The first cares of the minister were directed to engrossing the various governmental posts for his own creatures: this purpose, too little concealed, of necessity created dissatisfaction and distrust, and speedily resulted in a very general insurrection; and, within a brief period of the apparent full success of his iniquity, the Hindú vizir found his power limited to the walls of the citadel of the metropolis, in which he was now closely besieged. The sultan, too, his protégé, was also discovered to be seeking an opportunity of joining the adverse party. In this crisis, the vizir determined upon the murder of the sultan; but the latter receiving timely intimation of the design, was able to overpower the vizir's band with a well-prepared guard, and thus he met the fate he designed for his lord. Not long after this, the emperor began to give himself up to dissolute conduct, and, in consequence, the affairs of the kingdom quickly shewed the want of a master's hand. Added to the internal disorganisation, the empire suffered from the attacks of foreign enemies. Ibrahim of Jánpúr possessed himself of several districts bordering on his own dominions, and Mahmúd Khiljí of Malwa went so far as to make an attempt on the capital. To extricate himself from this pressing difficulty, the sultan called in the aid of one who was destined to play a prominent part in the history of his day, Behlól Lodí, at this time nominal governor, though virtual master of the dependencies of Lahore and Sirhind. By his assistance, the king was relieved from his immediate danger, and the protecting subject was dignified with the title of Khán Khánán (first of the nobles). Behlól's next appearance is in a somewhat altered character, as besieger of Delhí itself, and the adversary of the monarch he had lately saved: he was not however successful. Mohammed died in 849.

156.—Copper and silver mixed. 142 grs. Date 846.[26]

Obv.—سلطان محمد شاه بن فريد شاه بحضرت دهلي

R.—الخليفه امير المومنين خلدت خلافته ٨٤٦

157.—Copper. 85 grs. Date 842.[27]

Obv.—محمد شاه سلطاني

R.—دار الملك دهلي ٨٤٢

158.—Copper. 33½ grs.

Obv.—محمد شاه

R.—بحضرت دهلي

THIRTY-FIRST KING (A.H. 849—854; A.D. 1444—1450).

The Alá ud din bin Mohammed of the historians, who is entitled Alem Sháh on his own coins, succeeded his father. His accession was not, however, recognised by Behlól Lodí, whose obedience the new sultan was in no position to enforce. The first acts of the public life of this prince,

---

[26] The silver coin (No D.CC.XXVII., page 545) attributed by Marsden to this sultan, does not seem to be correctly assigned. The Devanágrí inscription on the obverse, connects the piece most distinctly with the type of money introduced about a century later by Shir Sháh, who is known to have remodelled the coinage, and whose style of coins is seen to be closely followed by his immediate successors, both in Hindústán and Bengal. The absence of the terms of filiation observable on the larger specimens of the undoubted coinage of Mohammed bin Ferid, in itself is sufficient to decide that the coin in question did not issue from his mint.

[27] Other coins of this type are dated, 843, 844, 847, 849 A.H.

clearly manifested to his subjects that they had little to expect either from his intellect or his conduct. In 851, Behlól Lodí made a second attempt on the city of Delhí, but with as little success as before; and shortly afterwards the sultan determined upon the unwise measure of removing his capital to Budaon: his motives for this change do not seem very obvious, as it was effected in the face of the advice of his whole court. It would appear as if he hoped for some fancied security which he did not feel at Delhí, to which the boundaries of so many adverse chiefs had attained a most inconvenient proximity. To complete his own ruin, the sultan allowed himself to be persuaded to disgrace his vizir, who, escaping to Delhí, quickly introduced the powerful Behlól Lodí, who at once, on becoming master of the capital, assumed the title of sultan;[28] somewhat strangely, however, retaining Alem Sháh's name in the Khutba. Not long after this, Alem Sháh offered to concede the empire to Behlól, on condition of being permitted to reside in peace at Budaon: no difficulty was made in taking advantage of this proposal; and from this time Behlól is reported to have rejected the name of Alem Sháh from the public prayers, and the latter was allowed to enjoy his insignificance undisturbed till his death in 883.

159. — Silver and copper. 146 grs. Date 853. R.

Obv.—سلطان عالمشاه بن محمد شاه

Sultan Alem Sháh, son of Mohammed Sháh.

R.—الخليفه امير المومنين خلد خلافته ۸۵۳

The Khalif, commander of the faithful. May his khalifat endure. 853.

---

[28] Behlól's actual accession is fixed, in the History of the Afghans, edited by Dorn, at 17th Rubí ul Awul, 855. Vide page 46. Edit. O. T. Fund.

160.—Copper. 66 grs. Date 853. R.

Obv.—عالمشاه سلطان

R.—٨٥٣ دار الملك دهلي

161.—Copper. 46 grs. R.

Obv.—سلطان عالمشاه بن محمد شاه بحضرت دهلي

R.— * * * الخليفه امير المومنين

One coin similar to No. 163 bears the figure 4 as the unit numeral of the date.

Thirty-Second King (A.H. 854—894; A.D. 1450—1488).

The vigorous rule of the Afghan Behlól Lodí offers a strong contrast to the inane weakness of the sway of the two Syuds who preceded him. His lengthened supremacy of thirty-eight years, however, affords but little of variety to dilate upon. The principal characteristics of his domination being defined in the successful and energetic subjection of his local governors, and a prolonged war, marked by the utmost determination on both sides, with the kings of Jánpúr: for a long time neither one party nor the other can be said to have obtained any very decided advantage, such as might have been expected to result from the great efforts made by both. The balance generally remained in favour of the monarch of Delhí; and at length, in the year 983, after a twenty-six years' war, he finally re-annexed the kingdom of Jánpúr to his own empire. It is recorded of this sultan, that, unlike Eastern monarchs in general, he was no respecter of pomps and ceremonies, remarking, "that it was enough for him that the world knew he was king, without his making a vain parade of royalty."

162.—Silver (impure). 142 grs. C.

Obv.—المتوكل الرحمن بهلول شاه سلطان بحضرت دهلي

The confiding-in-God, Behlól Sháh, the sultan.

R.—في زمن امير المومنين خلدت خلافته ٢ * *

In the time of the commander of the faithful. May his khalifat endure. * * 2.

163.—Silver and copper. 52 grs.

Obv.—بهلول شاه سلطان بحضرت دهلي

R.—الخليفه امير المومنين خلدت خلافته

164.—Copper. 85 grs. Date 855.

Obv.—بهلول شاه سلطان

R.—دار الملك دهلي ٨٥٥

165.—Copper. 67 grs. Date 886.

Obv.—Legend similar to No. 164.

R.—الخليفه - - ٨٨٦

166.—Copper.

Obv.—*Centre* بهلول شاه *Marg.*—السلطان

R.—نايب امير المومنين ٨٧٧

Dated coins of Behlól range from A.H. 855 to 893.

Thirty-Third King (A.H. 889—923; A.D. 1488—1517).

Some time before his decease, Behlól had nominated as his successor his son Nizám, who, accordingly, though not without opposition, ascended the imperial musnud under the title of Sekunder Sháh. In the division of his dominions in 883, the emperor had assigned the kingdom of of Jánpúr to his son Barbek. On attaining the supreme sovereignty, Sekunder demanded the nominal allegiance of his brother in the preliminary mention of his own name, in the public prayers recited in the portion of the country over which Barbek ruled: this being refused, it was found necessary to compel its concession by force of arms. In the action which ensued, Barbek was worsted, but was subsequently forgiven, and re-instated in his government. During the succeeding years, the sultan was occupied in the subjection of Sherif, which was effected in the capture of his stronghold Biana, and in the suppression of two somewhat formidable insurrections in Jánpúr and Oud. In 897, Sekunder extended his conquests over the whole of Behar, dispossessing Hussen, the last of the regal line of the Sherkí monarchs, who was forced to take refuge with Alá, king of Bengal: with this last the sultan of Delhí came to a satisfactory understanding, involving a mutual recognition of boundaries, etc. In 909, the emperor, for the first time, fixed his residence at Agrah, which henceforth was to supersede Delhí as the metropolis of Hindústán. Sekunder's rule was disgraced by an unusual display of bigotry, evidenced principally in a persevering destruction of Hindú temples, on the sites of which were raised Moslem mosques.

167.—Copper. 144 grs. Date A.H. 906. (Other dated coins have 896, 903, 906, and 918.)

Obv.—

المتوكل الرحمن سكندر شاه بهلول شاه سلطان بحضرت دهلي

R.— في زمن امير المومنين خلدت خلافته ٩٠٦

168.—Copper. 53 grs.

Obv.—المتوكل الرحمن سكندر شاه بهلول شاه

R.—امير المومنين خلدت خلافته * * *

THIRTY-FOURTH KING (A.H. 923—937; A.D. 1517—1530).

Ibráhím succeeded his father Sekunder; from the very commencement of his reign his arrogance disgusted the nobles of his own tribe of Lodí, who speedily sought to reduce his power by placing his brother, Jellál, on the throne of the kingdom of Jánpúr. Having compassed this purpose, however, some doubt arose as to the wisdom of their own act, and hence an attempt was made to weaken Jellál by the withdrawal of several Amrahs who had joined his standard. Jellál, detecting this design, determined upon active measures to secure himself; he therefore collected his forces and advanced to Kálpí, assuming the style of sultan, with the title of Jellál ud din. He next entered into negotiations with Azim Humáyún, who held Kalinjer for Ibráhím, and at length induced him to desert the cause of the emperor. Azim Humáyún failed at the time of need, and Jellál was reduced to a position of much difficulty, from which however he had a favourable opportunity of extricating himself, by the success of a sudden march upon Agrah, which he found almost undefended; but from some strange infatuation, he allowed himself to be deluded into treating with the governor of the city, and on the advance of Ibráhím, he was compelled to flee to Guálír, where he received a temporary shelter; he was, ultimately, after various adventures and escapes, captured and put to death.

The alarm excited by the unrestrained cruelties resulting from the distrustful disposition of the sultan, led to numerous other rebellions: among the rest, Deria Khán, viceroy of Behar, openly disclaimed allegiance; and his son, Mohammed, who succeeded him shortly after the commencement of the revolt, caused the Khutba to be read, and coin to be struck in his own name.[30] Daulat Lodí, the governor of part of the dependencies of Lahore, also rebelled, and solicited the protection of Báber, who had

---

[30] Ayin i Akberi.

already, in 930 A.H., taken possession of Lahore itself. Báber now sent an expedition under Alá, the brother of Ibráhím, but in the engagement which ensued, the army of the Moghuls was defeated with great slaughter. This was followed by the advance of Báber in person, and on the 7th of Rajab, 932, on the celebrated battle field of Paniput, Ibráhím, after an individually well-contested, though ill-directed action, lost his kingdom and his life.

169.—Copper. 83 grs. R.

Obv.—المتوكل الرحمن ابراهيم شاه سكندر شاه سلطان

R.—في زمن امير المومنين خلدت خلافته

170.—Copper. 37 grs. R.

Obv.—ابراهيم شاه سلطان

R.—امير المومنين خلدت خلافته

171.—Copper. 42 grs. R. Date 926.

Obv.—ابراهيم شاه سكندر * *

R.—امير المومنين خلدت خلافته ٩٢٦

THE MOGHUL CONQUEST.

The narrative of the chequered adventures of Báber and his son Humáyún is more pertinent to general history than a subject of peculiar import, in the present notices of the local succession of the Patán dynasty of Hindústán. It may, therefore, be sufficient to indicate more concisely than usual, the dates of the several prominent occurrences of the Indian reigns of these two monarchs.

Báber's sway, after his occupation of the cities of Delhí and Agrah, was not undisputed, but he may be said generally to have triumphed over all opposition: he died, in full possession of the empire of Hindústán, on 5th Jumád ul Awul, 936 A.H., and was succeeded by his son, Nasír ud din Humáyún. In 946, Hindal Mirza, another son of Báber, revolted; and shortly afterwards, Kámrán, the brother who held Kábul, followed his example, marching to Delhí, where he was met by Hindal, who persuaded him to join forces, and in company they advanced towards Agrah; but disagreeing by the way, Hindal, finding himself the weaker, fled, leaving Kamran to assume the imperial ensigns on his arrival at the capital. Humáyún was at this time engaged in a war with Shír Khán, who held a considerable portion of Bengal and Behar. On the 6th Safar, 946, Humáyún was surprised by his wily adversary, by whom he was totally routed, and his whole army destroyed. Humáyún himself, escaping with the utmost difficulty, joined his brothers at Agrah, who saw their common danger in the increasing power of Shír. For six months, consultations and disputes continued, which ended in the departure of Kámrán towards Kábul;[31] to this, succeeded the advance of Shír (now Shír *Sháh*); and Humáyún, after a temporary advantage, was finally defeated, in Muharrim, 947, the victor possessing himself of the capital. From this time until his triumphant re-conquest of his Indian empire in

---

31 Kámrán's coins are extant. The following is a description of a specimen in the East India Company's Collection. Kabul 947.

Silver. 71 grs.

Obv.—Area (diamond shaped) محمد کامران پادشاه غازي

Marg.—الملك السلطان الاعظم الخاقان خلد الله تعالي ملكه و سلطانه ضرب كابل سنه ٩٤٧

℞.—*Circular area*, the usual short symbol.

Marg.—ابابكر الصديق عمر الفاروق عثمان العون علي المرتضي

962, Humáyún was fated to be a wanderer: the tale of his sufferings, his escapes, his varied fortunes, and his prominent heroism, developed during this interval, forms a romance of kingly life but seldom equalled.

BABER.

172.—Silver. 71·5 grs. V.R.

Obv.—Centre ظهير الدين محمد بابر پادشاه

Zehír ud din Mohammed Baber Padshah.

Marg.—(worn) * * السلطان الاعظم

R.—*Centre* لااله الاالله محمد رسول الله

Marg.—علي المرتضي - - - -

* Ulí, the chosen!

173.—A second silver coin of Baber (E. I. Company's Cabinet), somewhat similar to the above, has the word غازي at the end of the inscription on the obverse area, in addition to the legend detailed under No. 172.

On the obverse margin is to be seen—الاعظم خاقان

R. *Area.*—As in the last coin.

Marg.—(Legible) العون علي المرتضي *

HUMAYUN.

174.—Gold. 13 grs. R.

Obv.—لا اله الا الله محمد رسول الله

R.—محمد همايون پادشاه غازي خلد الله ملكه

Mohammed Hamáyun Padshah Ghází. May God prolong his reign.

175.—Silver. 71 grs. R.

Obv.—Centre محمد همايون غازي

Mohammed Humáyun Ghází.

Marg.—الملك الامير السّلطان الاعظم الخاقان خلد الله تعالي ملكه و سلطانه ضرب اكره سنه ۹۴۴

The king, the amír, the most mighty sultan, the khákán. May Almighty God prolong his dominion and sovereignty. Struck at Agrah, year 944.

℞.—*Centre*

لااله الاالله محمّد رسول الله الله يرزق من يشاء بغير حساب

There is no god but God, Mohammed is the apostle of God. God is bountiful unto whom he pleaseth, without measure.

Marg.—بصدق ابابكر بعدل عمر بحياي عثمان بعلم علي رضي الله عنه

By the truth of Abubekir, by the justice of Umur, by the modesty of Usmán, by the wisdom of Alí, may God reward him.

176.—Another silver coin, 71 grs., struck at Agra, is dated 945. A variety, with a nearly square area, has the date 952; the name of the place of mintage is obliterated.

A fourth coin of the type here described, which is unfortunately wanting in both date and place of mintage, has the stamp or currency mark of Kamran; of this impression the following words are legible:—

عدل کامران پاد شاه غـ

Another silver coin of Humáyun (71 grains), has the محمّد همايون غازي only, in an oblong area. The reverse area being circular, as in the specimen engraved, the legend itself is confined to the usual short symbol. The margins are much worn, but apparently vary slightly in their legends from those of the above coins. There are traces of the figures 937.

Thirty-Sixth King (a.h. 947—952; a.d. 1540—1545).

Shír Sháh had already assumed the title of *Sháh* on his permanent subjection of Bengal; his entrance into Agrah, therefore, had to be signalised by no new accession of honorary designation. On attaining the supreme power in Hindústán, Shir's attention was directed to the due organisation of his kingdom in the more complete reduction of the Moghul governors of provinces, and the conquest of neighbouring states. In 948, he possessed himself of Malwa; in 949, he reduced the fort of Raisín, treacherously massacreing the garrison; in 951, he invaded and overran Marwar. His next exploit was the capture of Chitor, and his last operation the siege of Kalinjer, where he was killed by the explosion of a magazine in his own trenches, surviving only long enough to receive the report of victory, for which he had still sufficient life left to exclaim, "Thanks be to Almighty God." His rule was able and energetic, but deceitful. Of works of lasting value to his country, he is famed for having constructed a high road in extent *four* months' journey, from Bengal to Rohtas near the Indus. This undertaking was made complete by the caravanserais at each stage, and the excavation of wells at the distance of each mile and a half, the whole being planted with trees to afford shade to the traveller.

177.—Gold. 167 grs. U.

Obv.—لااله الاالله محمد رسول الله السلطان العادل

There is no god but God, Mohammed is the apostle of God. The just sovereign.

R.—شیرشاه السلطان خلد الله ملکه ۹۴۷ सा सर सही

Shir Sháh, the sultan. May God prolong his reign. 947. *Sā Săr Săhí.*

178.—Silver. 176 grs. Shirgurh, (9)49 A.H. (*Prinsep Coll.*)[32]

Obv.—Square area لااله الاالله محمد رسول الله

[32] The silver coin of a similar type to the above, described by Marsden under No. DCC.XXIX., as being dated 945, is not so dated

Marg.—ابابكر الصديق عمر الفاروق عثمان ذي النورين[33] على المرتضى

℞.—*Square area* شير شاه سلطان خلد الله ملكه

Marg.—श्री सेर साही

فريد الدنيا والدين ابوالمظفر ضرب شيركده ٩٤٩

179.—Silver. 175 grs. C.

Obv.—*Centre* لااله الاالله محمد رسول الله

Marg.—ابابكر عمر عثمان على السلطان العادل

Abábekir, Umur, Usmán, Ulí. The just sovereign.

℞.—*Centre* شيرشاه السلطان خلد الله ملكه و سلطانه ٩٤٩

Shir Sháh, the sultan. May God perpetuate his dominion and sovereignty. 949.

Marg.—श्री सेर साही فريد الدنيا والدين ابو المظفر جهانپناه

Feríd ud dunia u ud din, Abul Muzafar, Asylum of the world. *Sri Ser Sáhí.*

180.—Silver. 174 grs.

Obverse area and margin similar to No. 179.

℞.—*Centre* شير شاه سلطان خلد الله ملكه و سلطانه

Marg.—٩٥٢ श्री सेर साही فريد الدنيا و الدين ابو المظفر

---

in the only specimen of the kind in *his* cabinet in the British Museum. Marsden was unable to detect the Hindí inscription on the margin of the reverse of this medal, which, with the aid of a better specimen, such as the one now described, is clearly recognisable.

Marsden's No. DCC.XXXVII. is seen from *the* original coin to have been struck at گوالير Guálír, and not at Korah.

[33] ذي النورين *Possessor of two lights*, in reference to his marriage with two daughters of the prophet.

181.—Silver. 171·5 grs. C. (Date on a similar coin, 948.)
Obverse square area, as in gold coin No. 177.
Marg.—ابوبکر - عمر - عثمان - علی

R.—*Square area* ۹۴۹ شیرشاه السلطان خلد الله ملکه
श्री सेर साही
Marg.—ابوالمظفر والدین الدنیا فرید

182.—Silver. 175 grs. C.
The obverse square area contains the usual short symbol.
Marg.—ابابکرالصدیق عمرالخطاب - - علی المرتضی[34]

R.—*Square area* السلطان شیر شاه خلد الله ملکه
श्री सेर सह
Marg.—فریدالدین و الدنیا ابوالمظفر ضرب شیرکده - - -

183.—Silver. 175 grs. Struck at Kálpí.
Obv.—*Area* لااله الاالله محمد رسول الله ضرب کالپی

R.—*Area* सेर सहि شیرشاه سلطان خلد الله ملکه
Margins worn.

184.—Copper. 310 grs.
Obv.—۹۵۱ في عهد الامیراحامي فرید الدین الدنان
R.—ابو المظفرشیر شاه سلطان خلد الله ملکه

185.—Copper. 315 grs. Agrah, A.H. 950.
Obv.—*Area* ۹۵۰ في عهد الامیر الحامي
Marg.—السلطان العادل فرید الدین والدنیا
R.—*Area* شیر شاه سلطان ضرب اگره
Marg.—ابو المظفر خلدالله

186.—Copper. 316 grs.
Obv.—*Square area* سلطان شیر شاه خلد الله
Marg.—** ملکه وسلطنه الله

R.—*Square area* [35] فیعهد المیره الحالمی
Marg.—**۲ الله * *

---

[34] The eloquent. [35] Sic.

187.—Copper 310 grs. Similar to 186. ضرب گوالیر **Guálíer.**

188.—Copper. 151 grs.

Obv.—سلطان العادل ابو المظفر شیر شاه سلطان

R.— خلد الله ملکه و سلطانه *

189.—Copper. 43 grs.

Obv.— خلیفه الزمان السلطان

R.—٩٤٨ العادل شیر شاه سلطان

THIRTY-SEVENTH KING (A.H. 959—969; A.D. 1545—1553).

Adil Khán, the eldest son, was nominated successor of his father, Shir Sháh. Jellál Khán, the younger brother, however, taking advantage of his absence from the capital at the time of the death of the father, obtained possession of the imperial dignity under the title of Islám Shah; and not long afterwards, Adil made a formal resignation of his birthright, and saluted Islám Sháh as king, simultaneously accepting, for his own portion, the Jaghir of Bíána; but soon having cause to distrust the good faith of his brother, Adil fled to Mewat and openly revolted. This effort was quickly crushed by the sultan, and Adil took refuge in Behar, where all traces of his eventual fate are lost. This outbreak was followed by a second rebellion in the Punjáb, under Azim Humáyún, which was for the time subdued by the defeat of the insurgents. The rest of the reign of Islám was disturbed by repeated revolts, and during this latter period he had no less than three remarkable escapes from assassination. He died in 960 A.H.

190.—Silver. 168 grs. C.

Obv.—Square area - لا اله الا الله محمد رسول الله

Marg.—ابابکر الصدیق عمر الفاروق عثمان العون[35] علي المرتضي

Abúbekir the true, Umur the discerning, Usmán the defender, Ulí the chosen.

R.—*Marg.*

جلال الدنیا و الدین ابوالمظفر السلطان العادل ✡ ۹۷۷*

Jellal ud dunia wa ud din Abúl Muzafar, the just sovereign.

Area.—اسلام شاه ابن شیر شاه سلطان خلد الله ملکه ۹۵۴

श्री ईसलाम साहि

Islám Sháh, son of Shír Sháh the sultan. May God prolong his reign.

191.—Silver. 173 grs. (thick coin). C.

Obv.—*Area* لا اله الا الله محمد رسول الله

Marg.— - - - ابابکر و عمر و عثمان علي ضرب

R.—*Marg.* السلطان العادل ابو المظفر - - ین والدنیا سنه ۹۵۲

Area.— اسلام شاه ابن شیر شاه سلطان خلد الله ملکه

श्री इसलमसह

192.—Copper. 315 grs.

Obv.—في عهد الامیر الحامي * د* الدین الدنان

R.—ابو المظفر اسلام شاه سلطان بن شیرشاد خلد الله ملکه

193.—Copper. 38 grs.

Obv.—اسلم شاه شیر شاد سلطان

R.—خلیفه الزمان العادل

---

[35] The العون (The Defender, Patron, also *Servant*) is a somewhat doubtful reading, as on many coins there seems to be a dot over the third letter, making it الغون. Marsden has given this word as الفون, but the best cut specimens of Islám's mintage display the ع or غ in its perfect shape. Islám's coins are very uncertain in their orthography in other respects, the ابن being frequently written بن, and the साही Shahí, being used indiscriminately with साहि Shahī.

The same uncertain method of expressing the Devanagrí equivalent of the Persian name of شیرشاد is also to be seen in its full force on the coins of that prince.

Thirty-Eighth, Thirty-Ninth, and Fortieth Kings.

The historical events of the partial reigns of the three last of the Patán kings of the Delhí line, are so interwoven with one another, that it may be appropriate to notice them together. On Islám Sháh's death, his son, Firúz Khán, a boy of twelve years of age, was for the moment elevated to the throne of his father; but he was almost immediately murdered by Mubariz Khán, a nephew of Shír Sháh, who usurped the sovereignty, entitling himself Mohammed Adil Sháh. Equally infamous and ignorant, the self-elected king entrusted the direction of his kingdom to one Himú (a Hindú shopkeeper); fortunately the individual thus selected was as capable, as he subsequently proved himself courageous, and for a time upheld the monarch he served. The king's inconsistency in resuming jaghirs and governments from the holders and conferring them upon others, apparently without any object but to show his power so to do, led to an attack on his person in open court, from which, flight but narrowly saved him. In 961, a rebellion was organised, which obliged the monarch to march against the insurgents in person, when he attacked and routed them near Chunar. Shortly after this, Ibráhím Súr, Adil's cousin and brother-in-law, revolted, and took possession of Delhí and Agrah, obliging Adil to confine himself to the eastern portions of his dominions; no sooner, however, had Ibráhim seated himself on his newly erected throne, than another competitor started up in the person of Ahmed, a nephew of Shír Sháh, who, on this occasion, took the name of Sekunder Sháh, and defeating Ibráhím, succeeded to his lately acquired territories. In the meantime, Mohammed Khán Guria, governor of Bengal, rebelled against Mohammed Adil, but was eventually vanquished and slain by

Himú; prior to which last action, Humáyún had re-possessed himself of Agrah and Delhí, and thus in acquiring Sekunder's provinces found himself in antagonism with Mohammed Adil. Himú, hearing of the death of Humáyún, which occurred about this time, and leaving his master in safety at Clumar, advanced towards Agrah, which he entered unopposed, and thence proceeded to Delhí, where he overcame Tirdi Beg, the Moghul governor. He next prepared for a march on Lahore, but was met on the plain of Paniput by Behram, the guardian of the young prince Akber, and defeated and slain, after a display of considerable valour. Adil continued to reign in his Eastern dominions till he was killed, in 964, in a battle with Behadur Shah, a pretender to the throne of Bengal.

MOHAMMED ADIL.

194.—Silver. 174 grs. R.

Obv.—Square area لا اله الا الله محمد رسول الله

R.—*Square area* محمد عادل شاه سلطان خلد الله ملكه ٩٦١
श्री महमद सह

Mohammed Adil Sháh, sultan. May God prolong his reign. 961. *Srí Mahamad Sah.*

Margins illegible.

195.—Silver. V.R. As No. 194. Date 963.

196.—Copper. 308 grs. V.R.

Obv.—ابو المجاهد سلطان محمد شاه خلد الله ملكه

R.—في عهد الامير الحامي - دين و الد ٩٢١

SEKUNDER.

197.—Silver. 175 grs. U.

Obv.—Square area لا اله الا الله محمد رسول الله

R.—سلطان سكندر شاه سور - - ٩٦٢

Margins illegible.

198.—Copper. 35 grs. R.

Obv.—سلطان سکندر

R.—سکندر شاه ساطاني

The following account of the Oriental method of coining, as in use at Delhí in the time of Akber, may not be uninteresting, as evidencing the probable practice of the earlier period to which the coins of the present series more immediately refer.

The melter melts the refined plates of metal and casts them into *round* ingots. The zerrab cuts from the round ingots pieces of gold, silver, and copper, of the size of the coin. It is surprising, that in Irán and Turán, they cannot cut these round pieces without an anvil, made on purpose; and in Hindustan, the workman, without any such machine, performs this business with such exactness, that there is not the difference of a single hair. The seal-engraver engraves the dies of coins on steel and such like metals. The sickchy places the round piece of metal between two dies, and, by the strength of the hammerer, both sides are stamped at one stroke.

Rupeeah روپیه, is a silver coin of a round form, in weight 11¼ mashahs. It was first introduced in the time of Shir Khán, and under the present reign it has been revived, and made more pure. —*Gladwin's Ayin Akberi.*

In preference to complicating the text with multitudinous references to similar coins, varying from the specimens described, only in date, it has been deemed advisable to subjoin, in a distinct form, a comprehensive Table, embracing all the annual dates obtainable from a careful examination of the contents of the various cabinets, that have contributed materials for the foregoing review of the moneys of the kings of Delhí.

The numbers printed in larger type refer to the coins which are to be found described at large in the text. The ordinary numerals imply only a general identity in the piece bearing the date, with the coin to which the number itself properly belongs in the preceding detail. It has not been so much an object to make the present summary an exposition of the different extant species of coins, as to indicate, in a connected form, the years capable of citation as those comprised in the reign of certain given monarchs, proved by their coins. The abbreviations, B.M., I.H., M., P., refer to the various collections of the British Museum, the East India House, and the accumulations of Marsden and Prinsep, both of which last are now deposited in our National Museum. Where no such acknowledgment is appended, the examples have been taken from coins in the author's own possession.

ABSTRACT TABLE OF DATES.

	Gold and Silver.	Billon and Copper.
Mohammed bin Sam.		
590	2 I.H.	
id.	G 2 I.H.	
596	**1**	
id.	2 I.H.	
598	3	
Altumsh.		
623		**14**
Masáud.		
641	**33**	
Mahmúd.		
654	39	
657	39	
658	**39**	
662	39	
Balbán.		
664	42	
665	42	
669	42	
673	**42**	
674	42 B.M.	
678	*b.*	
Kaikobád.		
687	**46**	
688	46 M.	
Fírúz.		
691	50	
694	50	
695	**50**	
Ibrahím.		
695	**54**	
Alá ud din.		
699	57 B.M.	
700		60
702		**59**, 60
703	57 M.	59
704	G. *c.* B.M.	60
705	57 I.H.	60
707		60
710	57	**60**
[1] 711	57 M.	59 I.H.
712	**57**	59
713	57 B.M.	59
714	57 B.M.	59
715	57 B.M.	59

	Gold and Silver.	Billon and Copper.
Umur.		
715		**63**
Mubárik.		
716	64 B.M.	66
717	**64**	**67**
718	**65**	**68, 69**
719		69
720		70
Khusrú.		
720		{ **74** Cast No. 8 }
Tughlak I.		
720		79
721	**75**	**80**
722	77	80
723	78	80
724	**78**	80
725		80
Mohammed Tughlak.		
725	**87**	
726	**82**	
727	**83**	
728	**88**	
729	89	
730	**89**	
Brass Tokens. { 730		{ **96, 101, 105**
731		**97**
732 }		**98**
732	**93**	
733	**94**	93
734	93	93
735	92	93, 94
736	**84**	93
737	94	
738		94
741	[2]	
742	**85**	
743	**95**	
748		**110, 111**
749	110 I.H.	
Fírúz III.		
759		115
761		115 I.H.
766		115 I.H.
767		115
769		115 I.H.
770		115
771		115

	Gold and Silver.	Billon and Copper.
Fírúz III. (Continued.)		
772		115 I.H.
773		**115**
775		115
776		115 I.H.
777		115
778		115 A.S.[4]
779		115
780		115
783		115
784		**118**
787		118
788	114	118
789		118
Fírúz & Ziffer.		
791		**129**
Tughlak II.		
790		**126**
Abúbekir.		
791		**129**
792		129
793		129
Nasir ud din Mohammed.		
790	**135**	136
793		**136**
794		136
Sekunder.		
795		{ **140**, **141**, **142** }
Násir ud din Mahmúd.		
795	144	
796	**144**	
797 }		{ Nuserut, **150**
798 }		151 }
800		147
801		147
803 [3]		Fírúz.
804 [3]		id.
807		{ Nuserut, **151** }
813		**145**
815		**147**
816 }		{ Fírúz, **122**
818 }		**123** }

	Gold and Silver.	Billon and Copper.
Mubárik II.		
832		**154**
833		154
834		153
835		153
836		154
Mohammed bin Ferid.		
842		**157**
843		156
844		157
846		**156**
847		157
848		156
Alem Sháh.		
853		{ **159**, **160** }
Behlól Lodí.		
855		**164**
858		162
860	162	162
863		164
866		164
868		164
873		164
877		**166**
886		**165**
888		166 B.M.
889		165
890	162	
893		165
Sekunder Behlól.		
895		167 M.
904		167 B.M.
906		167
909		167 B.M.
914		167 B.M.
915		167
916		167 B.M.
918		167 B.M.
919		167 B.M.
Ibráhím.		
926		**171**
Humáyún.		
937 ?	176	
944 *Agrah.*	**175**	
945 *id.*	**176**	
952 ?	176	

	Gold and Silver.	Billon and Copper.
Shír Shah.		
946	181 [5]	
947	**177**	
948	181 [6]	**189**
949	**178, 179**	
950	180 B.M.	**185**
951	180 B.M.	**184**
952	**180**	**186**
Islám Sháh.		
952	**191**	
953	190	
954	**190**	192
955	190 I.H.	
956	191	
957	190 [6]	
958	190	
959	190	
960	190 [6]	
Mohammed Adil.		
961	**194**	**196**
963	**195**	
Sekunder.		
962	**197**	

[1] Struck بدارالاسلام

[2] Fraehn, "Recensio," p. 177.

[3] Page 67.

[4] Asiatic Society.

[5] See also Marsden's plates, Fig. DCC.XXX.

[6] See Cast Types.

APPENDIX.

In closing this description of the various coins of the Patán kings of Delhí, it may be useful to append a brief *résumé* of the more prominent changes, which an exact examination of the series of their medals has rendered requisite in the list of the accessions of the different sovereigns quoted at the head of this essay. Though some apology is due for the position in which these rectifications appear, yet the present allocation has been the almost necessary result of the mode in which these notes have been written and published; that is to say, in detached portions: the major part of the subject having been undertaken at the moment, by instalments; as the more locally interesting claims on the space of the Journal in which these descriptions were to appear admitted of their publication. Hence, as it was requisite to adopt some distinct groundwork whereon to proceed, the recognised list, and the hitherto received statements of Ferishtah, were accepted in the first instance as safe bases, from which any important divergence was deemed improbable. This expectation will be seen to have been erroneous in the following instances :—

No. 15	Umur . . .	for 716	read 715.	See coin 63, and note p. 73.
16	Mubarik . .	— 717	— 716.	—— 66.[1]
17	Khusrú . .	— 721	— 720.	—— 74, and cast No. 8.
18	Tughlak . .	— 721	— 720.	—— 79.
24	Sekunder .	— 796	— 795.	—— 140, 141, 142.
25	Mahmud's death	814	— 815.	See note, p. 76.

The last point in this detail has been sufficiently explained in a note at the foot of page 73; but the other discrepancies seem to require a few additional remarks, not so much on account of any difficulty existing in the questions themselves, as from the curious exactitude with which the proposed emendations frequently support one another. The conflicting nature of the historical dates, and the testimony of coins Nos. 66 and 74, formed the subject of notice in their fit place; but the precise nature of the numeral on coin No. 63, having escaped detection at the right moment, necessitated a correction, which will be found in the note to coin No. 140. It now merely remains to direct attention to these consecutive evidences, and to express a conviction, which isolated unsupported medals might not have altogether justified, that the

[1] The date of 716, to be found on this coin, is supported by a like figured date on a similar coin in the East India House Cabinet, and is conclusively confirmed by the *written* inscription of the same date on a silver coin of Mubarik in the British Museum. (See cast No. 6.)

Mohammedan authors, who assign the several dates of 716,[2] 717, and 721,[3] as the epochs of accession of the respective princes noted above, are one and all incorrect, to the extent of having post-dated each of these different events by one year. The writers in question seem to have adhered with sufficient apparent scruple to the correct duration of the reign of each monarch; but by some error in the earlier part of their narrations, they have been led into a series of mistakes, which their tests of accuracy proved insufficient to rectify. Having advanced thus far in the correction of Ferishtah's erroneous dates, and having ante-dated a succession of three kings each by one year, the application of a similar process in favor of the next monarch in order is easily justified; especially as his predecessor, who ascended the throne in the third month of the Mohammedan year, reigned somewhat less than five months: whence it is manifest, that in accepting these last data[4] the elevation of the successor must of necessity be placed in the same year.

This point has been made the subject of separate mention, for the purpose of drawing more direct attention to the question involved in its admission, namely, the value of the figure o which is to be found in the unit place of the annual date on coin No. 79. As long as Ferishtah's dates remained unimpugned, it was imperative to conclude that this numeral was, in its position on this coin, intended to represent a five; as a monarch who was asserted to have attained his throne in 721, and retained it till 725, had obviously no year of his sway which would answer to the employment of a final naught in the notification of the period of issue of any of his coins. Having, however, seen cause to discredit so much of the historian's testimony, it may now be permissible to restore the hitherto questionable figure to its correct place in the list of numerals, and to account it a naught and nothing but a naught.[5]

In arriving at this determination of the functions of the dubious figure, it is requisite, before finally taking leave of this question, to anticipate a notice pertinent thereto, in its due dynastical order,

---

[2] Assistance in the due assignment of the disputed date of the accession of any given king, is naturally to be sought in the determination of the epoch of the inauguration of his predecessor and the length of his reign. There are discrepancies as to the æra of Alá ud din's enthronement to the amount of one year; or, more correctly speaking, a difference between the citation of the year 695 (Mirát ul Alem and Tubkát Akberi) and 696 (Ferishtah). The duration of his rule is pretty uniformly fixed at 20 years and some months.

[3] The Tubkát Akberi gives 720 as the date of the accession of Ghiás ud din Tughlak.

[4] Strange as it may seem, it is to be borne in mind that the dates of the months are often perfectly trustworthy, when the simultaneously appended year is altogether false.

[5] See note to coin No. 74, and coin No. 135.

and to rectify in this place the opinion expressed in regard to the date and circumstances under which the coin (No. 135) bearing the joint names of Fírúz and his son Mohammed was issued: it will be observed that, all doubt having now been removed as to the fact of its true date being "790 A.H.," it can only be looked upon as a medal of the regency of the son, struck during the temporary retirement of the father from the cares of state; and not, as was at one time supposed, a simple medal of the son, coined after his full accession to the undivided throne of Delhí.

Continuing the examination of the various dates pertaining to the sway of the remaining monarchs, it would seem that the error which extended itself to the epochs of the inauguration of four kings in succession, was by some means accommodated in the accurate assignment of the æra of the commencement of the rule of Mohammed bin Tughlak: but again, in the date of the installation of Alá ud din Sekunder Sháh, there recurs a similar inaccuracy of one year, as it is clear from the many dated coins of this prince, that the 45 days of his rule should be assigned to the year 975, and not to 976,[6] as affirmed by Ferishtah. (See coins No. 140, 141, 142, etc.) This error, in as far as its results might have affected the accessions of the monarchs who follow, will be seen to have been speedily and successfully got rid of by the perpetration of a new error, which curtailed the full extent of the reign of Mahmúd, Sekunder's immediate successor, by the identical overdrawn year.

In addition to the above rectifications of the inaccuracies of Eastern historical authorities, there are errors to be acknowledged as the writer's own, as well as many slight orthographical discrepancies in the Anglicised Oriental names, arising from the occasional correction of the press by other hands during the temporary absences of the author. The latter, where considered of sufficient consequence, will be found duly recorded in the list of errata. The former demand a more explicit notice, and may briefly be enumerated as follows:—

1st. The incorrect assignment of the coin described under No. 58, which is shown, from a more extended examination of the medals of other Indian dynasties, to have belonged to Alá ud din Mohammed Sekunder al Sání, of Khwárizm, who conquered Ghazní in 612 A.H.,[7] and not to Alá ud din Mohammed Sekunder al Sání of Delhí.

2nd. The omission of an important variety of the binominal coins of Fírúz III., which, had they not escaped notice, should have appeared after coin No. 123. These medals bear the joint

[6] The Tubkát Akberi also assigns 976 (19th Rabí al Awal) as the date of the inauguration of Sekunder.

[7] Abúl Faraj, De Guignes, etc.

names of Fírúz and his son Futteh Khán. They are sufficiently common, and in the obvious variation in the form of the letters of the legends, from those of the metropolitan monies of the father, and the inferiority of their execution as works of art, indicate themselves the produce of a provincial mint.

The following is all that can be satisfactorily deciphered of the inscriptions:—

Silver and copper. 135 grs.

Obv.— * * فتحخان فيروز شاه

R.—ضرب في زمن امير المومنين ابوالفتح خلدت خلافته

Others have the name of the khalif عبدالله in the place of ابوالفتح

Advantage has been taken of the existence of sundry unpublished casts of rare coins, prepared to be used as types by the late James Prinsep, which have lately passed into the possession of the trustees of the British Museum, to add to the numismatic illustrations already afforded by the copper-plate engravings which elucidate the subject-matter of the present notice. Referring to the detailed transcripts of the legends of the several medals embodied in the preceding pages, it will be sufficient for the explanation of the subjoined impressions, to indicate generally the class to which each specimen belongs, adding merely the date or other variation in which their originals may have differed from the coins described at large in the text.

No. 1. Cast of the original coin described at the foot of p. 17.
2. Ditto ditto of No. 27.
3. A coin of Kaikobád, similar to No. 46.
4. An imperfect specimen of Alá ud din's gold coinage, No. [c] 57.
5. Mubarik Sháh, [d] 65.
6. Idem, similar to 64, but dated 716 A.H.
7. Behádúr Sháh بهادرشاه السلطان بن سلطان p. 42, 43.
8. Khusrú, similar to No. 74, but the cast of a *different* coin A.H. 720 (٧٢٠)
9. Tughlak Sháh, similar to 75.
10. Mohammed Tughlak, from a gold coin similar to No. 82.
11. Idem id. id. No. 84.
12. Surfaces of different coins { To the right, the reverse of a coin similar to No. 88. To the left, the reverse of a coin similar to No. 96.
13. Shír Sháh, similar to No. 181, with the addition of وسلطانه in the reverse area. A.H. 948.
14. Shír Sháh, similar to No. 179.
15. Islám Sháh, similar to No. 190. Date 960.
16. Islám Sháh, idem. Date 957.

ADDENDA ET CORRIGENDA.

Page 5, line 12, for بسنه ستة read سنه ست

,, 15, coin 14, for "Silver" read "Silver and copper."

,, 21, line 18, for "Balbam" read "Balban."

,, 22, coin [a], for "Copper" read "Silver."

,, 23, line 20, for "688" read "658."

,, 25, line 7, after "and" insert "one of his commanders."

,, — coin 42, for "Date 678" read "673;" and alter Arabic accordingly.

,, 29, note [8], and page 58, line 19, *et seq.*, for "Akhberí" read "Akberí."

,, 55, coin 94, obverse, add الكريم

,, — —— reverse, for شنه read سنه

,, 63, coin 111, for "109," read "110."

,, 66, coin 118, for "114" read "115."

,, 72, coin 136, for "795" read "790."

,, 100, line 6, for "Clumar" read "Chunar."

COINS OF THE PATAN SULTANS OF HINDOSTAN.

J. Basire del. et sc.

COINS OF THE PATAN SULTANS OF HINDOSTAN.

COINS OF THE PATAN SULTANS OF HINDOSTAN.

COINS OF THE PATAN SULTANS OF HINDOSTAN.

Pl. V.

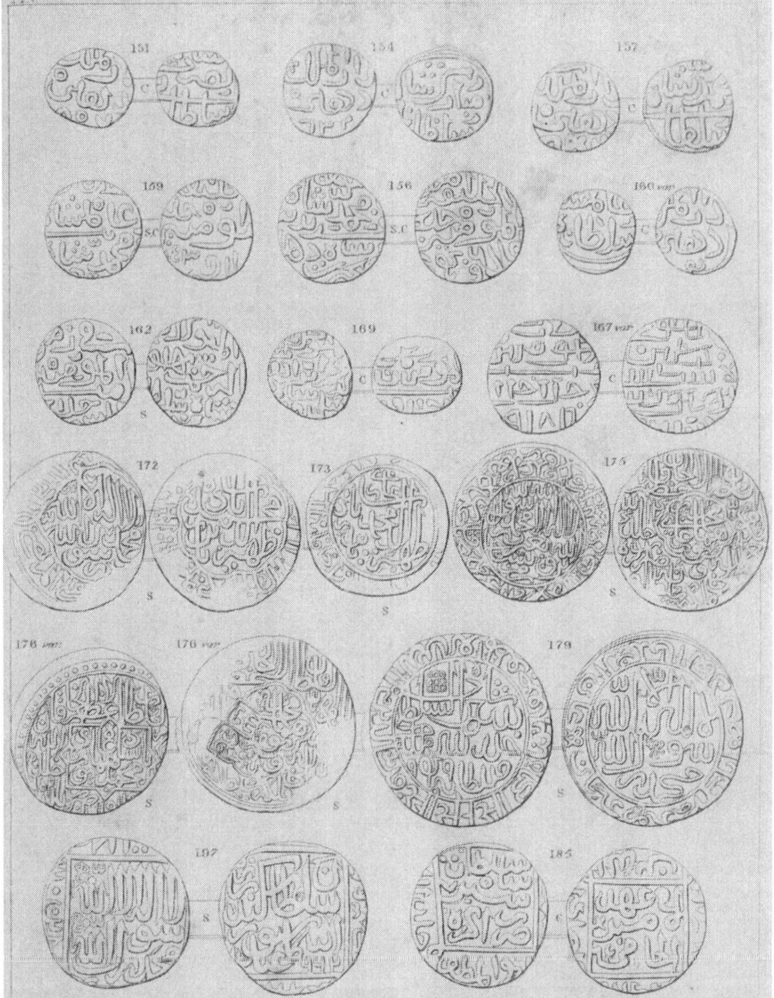

COINS OF THE PATAN SULTANS OF HINDOSTAN.

1. S.

2. S.

3. S.

4. G.

5. G.

6. S.

7. S.

8. C.

9. G.

14. S.

15. S.

12. B.

13. S.

10. G.

11. G.

16. S.